LifeChange
S E R I E S

NAVPRESS ®
A MINISTRY OF THE NAVIGATORS
P.O. Box 6000, Colorado Springs, CO 80934

© 1987 by The Navigators
All rights reserved, including translation
ISBN: 0-89109-068-1
10686

Printed in the United States of America

CONTENTS

Volume One

ACKNOWLEDGMENTS

This LIFECHANGE study has been produced through the coordinated efforts of a team of Navigator Bible study developers and NavPress editorial staff, along with a nationwide network of fieldtesters.

SERIES EDITOR: KAREN HINCKLEY

HOW TO USE THIS STUDY

Most guides in the LIFECHANGE series of Bible studies cover one book of the Bible. Because it is hard to study more than one chapter of a Gospel at a time and because Luke includes many of Jesus' words and deeds that Matthew and Mark omit, we've divided this study of Luke's Gospel into two volumes. The first covers Jesus' birth, youth, baptism, and ministry in Galilee. The second volume begins as Jesus trains His disciples during a journey toward Jerusalem, and it ends with His trial, death, and resurrection.

Objectives

Although the LIFECHANGE guides vary with the individual books they explore, they share some common goals:

1. To provide you with a firm foundation of understanding and a thirst to return to each book;

2. To teach you by example how to study a book of the Bible without structured guides;

3. To give you all the historical background, word definitions, and explanatory notes you need, so that your only other reference is the Bible;

4. To help you grasp the message of each book as a whole;

5. To teach you how to let God's Word transform you into Christ's image.

Each lesson in this study is designed to take 60 to 90 minutes to complete on your own. The guide is based on the assumption that you are completing one lesson per week, but if time is limited you can do half a lesson per week or whatever amount allows you to be thorough.

Flexibility

LIFECHANGE guides are flexible, allowing you to adjust the quantity and depth of your study to meet your individual needs. The guide offers many optional questions in addition to the regular numbered questions. The optional questions, which appear in the margins of the study pages, include the following:

Optional Application. Nearly all application questions are optional; we hope you will do as many as you can without overcommitting yourself.

For Thought and Discussion. Beginning Bible students should be able to handle these questions, but even advanced students need to think about them. These questions frequently deal with ethical issues and other biblical principles. They often offer cross-references to spark thought, but the references do not contain obvious answers. These questions are good for group discussions.

For Further Study. These questions include: a) cross-references that shed light on a topic the book discusses, and b) questions that delve deeper into the passage. You can omit them to shorten a lesson without missing a major point of the passage.

(Note: You are given the option of outlining the book as you go along. Although the outline is optional, you will almost surely find it worthwhile. If you prefer, outline the book at the end of your study.)

If you are meeting in a group, decide together which optional questions to prepare for each lesson and how much of the lesson you will cover at the next meeting. Normally, the group leader should make this decision, but you might let each member choose his own application questions.

Sometimes there is space in the margins of the study guide to jot answers to optional questions or notes from your discussion. However, you will often want more space for such notes. You can use blank pages between lessons and at the end of the guide for notes, or you can begin a separate Bible study notebook. A separate notebook will give you plenty of room to answer optional questions, record prayer requests and answers to prayer, write notes from discussions, plan applications and record results, and describe experiences in your life that are teaching you spiritual lessons. A notebook like this can be invaluable.

As you grow in your walk with God, you will find the LIFECHANGE guide growing with you—a helpful reference on a topic, a continuing challenge for application, a source of questions for many levels of growth.

Overview and details

The guide begins with an overview of the book. The key to interpretation is context—what is the whole passage or book about?—and the key to context is purpose—what is the author's aim for the whole work? In lesson one you will lay the foundation for your study by asking yourself, Why did the author (and God) write the book? What did he want to accomplish? What is the book about?

Then, in lesson two, you will begin analyzing successive passages in detail. You'll interpret particular verses in light of what the whole paragraph is about, and paragraphs in light of the whole passage. You'll consider how each passage contributes to the total message of the book. (Frequently reviewing an outline of the book will enable you to make these connections.) Then, once you understand what the passage says, you'll apply it to your own life.

In lesson twelve, at the end of both Part One and Volume One, you will review what Jesus has revealed so far about His and the disciples' missions in the world. Then in Volume Two, you will study the second half of Jesus' ministry. Finally, in lesson twenty-nine you will review the whole Gospel of Luke, returning to the big picture to see whether your view of it has changed after closer study. Review will also strengthen your grasp of major issues and give you an idea of how you have grown from your study.

Kinds of questions

Bible study on your own—without a structured guide—follows a progression. First you *observe*: What does the passage say? Then you *interpret*: What does the passage mean? Lastly you *apply*: How does this truth affect my life? The act of wording a question for the guide nearly always makes it interpretation, however, so you may want to observe first yourself.

Some of the "how" and "why" questions will take some creative thinking, even prayer, to answer. Some are opinion questions without clear-cut right answers; these will lend themselves to discussions and side studies.

Don't let your study become an exercise of knowledge alone. Treat the passage as God's Word, and stay in dialogue with Him as you study. Pray, "Lord, what do you want me to see here?" "Father, why is this true?" "Lord, how does this apply to my life?"

It is important that you write down your answers. The act of writing clarifies your thinking and helps you remember.

Study Aids

A list of reference materials, including a few notes of explanation to help you make good use of them, begins on page 151 for Volume One. This guide is designed to include enough background to let you interpret with just your Bible and the guide. Still, if you want more information on a subject or want to study a book on your own, try the references listed.

Scripture versions

Unless otherwise indicated, the Bible quotations in this guide are from the *New International Version of the Bible*. Other versions cited are the *Revised Standard Version* (RSV), the *New American Standard Bible* (NASB), and the *King James Version* (KJV).

Use any translation you like for study, preferably more than one. A paraphrase, such as *The Living Bible*, is not accurate enough for study, but it can be helpful for comparison or devotional reading.

Memorizing and meditating

A psalmist wrote, "I have hidden your word in my heart that I might not sin against you" (Psalm 119:11). If you write down a verse or passage that challenges or encourages you, and reflect on it often for a week or more, you will find it beginning to affect your motives and actions. We forget quickly what we read once; we remember what we ponder.

When you find a significant verse or passage, you might copy it onto a card to keep with you. Set aside five minutes during each day just to think about what the passage might mean in your life. Recite it over to yourself, exploring its meaning. Then, return to your passage as often as you can during the day for a brief review. You will soon find it coming to mind spontaneously.

For group study

A group of four to ten people allows the richest discussions, but you can adapt this guide for other sized groups. It will suit a wide range of group types, such as home Bible studies, growth groups, youth groups, and businessmen's studies. Both new and experienced Bible students, new and mature Christians, will benefit from the guide. You can omit or leave for later any questions you find too easy or too hard.

The guide is intended to lead a group through one lesson per week. However, feel free to split lessons if you want to discuss them more thoroughly. Or, omit some questions in a lesson if preparation or discussion time is limited. You can always return to this guide for personal study later on. You will be able to discuss only a few questions at length, so choose some for discussion and others for background. Make time at each discussion for members to ask about anything that gave them trouble.

Each lesson in the guide ends with a section called "For the group." These sections give advice on how to focus a discussion, how you might apply the lesson in your group, how you might shorten a lesson, and so on. The group leader should read each "For the group" at least a week ahead so that he or she can tell the group how to prepare for the next lesson.

Each member should prepare for a meeting by writing answers for all the background and discussion questions to be covered. If the group decides not to take an hour per week for private preparation, then expect to take at least two meetings per lesson to work through the questions. Application will be very difficult, however, without private thought and prayer.

Two reasons for studying in a group are accountability and support. When each member commits in front of the rest to seek growth in an area of life, you can pray with one another, listen jointly for God's guidance, help one another to resist temptation, assure each other that the other's growth matters to you, use the group to practice spiritual principles, and so on. Pray about one another's commitments and needs at most meetings. Spend the first few minutes of each meeting sharing any results from applications prompted by previous lessons. Then discuss new applications toward the end of the meeting. Follow such sharing with prayer for these and other needs.

If you write down each other's applications and prayer requests, you are more likely to remember to pray for them during the week, to ask about them at the next meeting, and to notice answered prayers. You might want to get a notebook for prayer requests and discussion notes.

Notes taken during discussion will help you remember, follow up on ideas, stay on the subject, and clarify a total view of an issue. But don't let notetaking keep you from participating. Some groups choose one member at each meeting to take notes. Then someone copies the notes and distributes them at the next meeting. Share these tasks so that everyone will feel included and no one will feel burdened. Some groups have someone take notes on a large pad of paper or erasable marker board (preformed shower wallboard works well), so that everyone can see what has been recorded.

Page 154 lists some good sources of counsel for leading group studies. *The Small Group Letter*, published by NavPress, is unique, offering insights from experienced leaders each month.

Map of Palestine in Jesus' Time

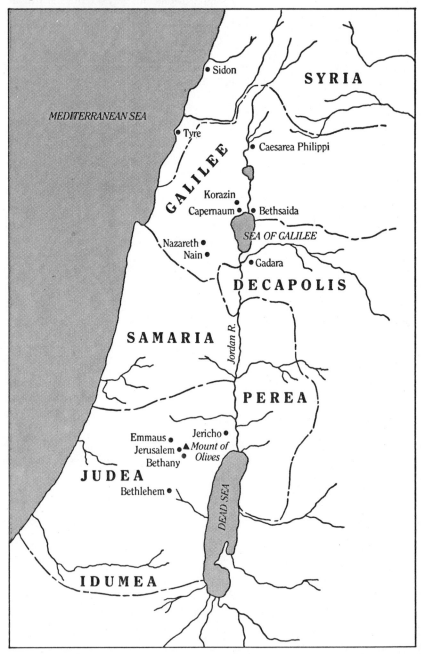

LUKE AND HIS GOSPEL

A Gospel

Gospel is an Old English word that means "good news." It translates the Greek word *euangelion* (*eu-*, "good" and *angelion*, "message"), which also gives us words like "evangelist" and is related to words like "angel."

When the first Christians wanted to record the "good news" about the Man who was God, none of the familiar forms of literature seemed suitable. The Christians didn't write the kinds of biographies or sacred texts that were common in Greek, Roman, or Jewish culture. Instead, they created a new form: the Gospel.

The Gospels were composed of scenes and sayings from Jesus' life remembered by His disciples and passed on, probably word for word. Oriental disciples learned by committing their masters' words and actions to memory for imitation. As Leon Morris notes, "rabbis used to cast their teaching into forms suitable for memorization and insist that their pupils learn it by heart."[1] The apostles faithfully recalled both individual statements and the overall progress of Jesus' time with them.

Luke said that by the time he wrote his Gospel, "Many have undertaken to draw up an account of the things that have been fulfilled among us . . ." (Luke 1:1). Apparently, other Christians had begun to record what the apostles remembered of Jesus' words and deeds. The Gospel of Mark may have been among several written sources Luke had available when he wrote his "orderly account" (Luke 1:3) of Jesus' ministry. Luke was also able to speak to people who had known Jesus (see "Physician and writer" on page 12).

Four Gospels

Many collections of Jesus' words and deeds were composed in the first century after His death, but God uniquely inspired four men to write the Gospels that would bear His authority. Why four? We can speculate, or we can simply

11

be glad for all four masterful portraits that reveal Our Lord in different lights. As J. Sidlow Baxter asks, which of the four could we do without?[2]

It is striking how coherent a picture of a single man and a single set of events emerges from four such different points of view. Observe the distinct interests and emphases in these examples:

1) To Matthew, who writes for Jewish Christians, Jesus is above all the King of David's line promised in the Hebrew Scriptures and the Teacher who brings a new revelation of God's Law. Matthew weaves fulfillments of Old Testament prophecies around five discourses about the Law and the Kingdom.

Mark pens a short Gospel in quick scenes that drive toward the Cross, revealing the Christ more in works of power and service than in words of wisdom.

John records a few miraculous signs and several long discourses to spark faith in God the Son.

And finally, Luke crafts his account of the Son of Man, the Savior of the World, to be both meticulously accurate and also captivating for a cultured Greek audience.

2) John begins with Jesus' pre-existence as God, and Mark starts with Jesus' baptism as an adult. Neither tells of Jesus' birth or lineage. Matthew opens with a genealogy that traces down from Abraham (the father of the Israelite covenant), David (the head of the Jewish royal line), and Joseph (Jesus' legal father in Jewish eyes, though not His natural one). Matthew's birth account focuses on kingship and prophecy. By contrast, Luke narrates the birth with warm, human touches, and he traces Jesus back to Adam—the father of Jew and Gentile—and then to God. Matthew's Jewish-minded nativity focuses on men, but Luke delights in pregnant women and old widows.

3) John highlights Jesus' ministry in Jerusalem. Matthew and Mark describe mainly His Galilean ministry and His last week in Jerusalem. But Luke includes ten long chapters in which Jesus journeys toward Jerusalem, training His disciples. We call Matthew, Mark, and Luke the *synoptic* (one view) Gospels because they have much more material in common than any of them has with John. However, Luke's journey to Jerusalem includes at least thirty incidents, parables, and sayings that Matthew and Mark omit.

As you study Luke's Gospel, we will point out more features that mark its unique contribution to the Scripture.

Physician and writer

Luke was Paul's "beloved physician" (Colossians 4:14). He traveled with Paul on the apostle's second missionary journey. When Paul reached Philippi, Luke probably remained there (Acts 16:10-17) and some years later left Philippi with Paul (Acts 20:6-38). Luke went with Paul to Palestine (Acts 21:1-18) and stayed for some time with Philip the evangelist in Caesarea.

When Paul was arrested in Jerusalem and sent prisoner to Rome, Luke accompanied him (Acts 27:1-28:16). These travels gave Luke opportunities to meet many of Jesus' original disciples and eyewitnesses to His life, and also to absorb Paul's understanding of the Savior of all people. Because Luke recorded several events in Mary's life that the other Gospels do not include, many people suspect that Luke may have spoken with her about her Son.

Although Luke was present at some of the events he recorded in the Acts of the Apostles, he was not an eyewitness of anything in his Gospel (Luke 1:2-3). We believe he was born a Gentile, but he may have become a Jew before he heard of Christ. Luke was steeped in the urban, Gentile (non-Jewish), Greek-speaking culture of the Roman Empire; the prologue to his Gospel shows that he could write literary Greek when he chose. Also, Luke was well versed in the *Septuagint,* the Greek translation of the Old Testament that Jews all over the Empire used.

We can sometimes detect signs of Luke's training as a physician in the details he chose to include. When recounting healing miracles, for example, he used technical Greek medical words to describe the ailment (5:12, 14:2), while Matthew and Mark used laymen's terms. Luke included sayings in which Jesus compared Himself to a physician (4:23, 5:31) that the other Gospels omitted, but in 8:43 he omitted the fact that the bleeding woman spent all her money on doctors to no avail (Mark 5:26). Luke was especially fond of the words *salvation* and *saved,* which in Greek also meant *healing* and *healed* (1:71; 2:30; 7:50; 8:36,48,50; 9:1-2,42; 17:19; 19:9-10; 23:35-39). Finally, the physician used his skills of minute observation and interview to give us precise accounts of many events.

When Luke wrote

Dates for Luke's Gospel vary. Leon Morris favors the early 60s AD, since Acts ends abruptly in 62 AD and nothing in either book demands a later date.[3] I. Howard Marshall leans toward a date shortly before or after 70 AD, noting Luke's interest in Jesus' prophecies of the destruction of Jerusalem, fulfilled in 70 AD.[4] Dates as late as 110 AD have been suggested.

Theophilus

Luke's Gospel is the longest book in the New Testament. At that time, books were hand-written on scrolls of papyrus reed, and a papyrus scroll could scarcely have been made longer without falling apart. But despite its length, Luke's Gospel must have intrigued its literary Greek audience.

The book is addressed to "Theophilus" (1:3), which means "lover of God." Luke may have made up a name to symbolize all those who would come to his book to learn about Jesus. However, it was common in Luke's day to write for and dedicate to a wealthy patron, who helped pay for publishing the book. Theophilus was a common Greek name, and this man may have been an educated Gentile aristocrat, either a new convert or an inter-

13

ested pagan. Unlike Matthew, Luke made a point of explaining Jewish practice and events so as to help a Gentile understand them.[5]

1. Leon Morris, *The Gospel According to Saint Luke* (Grand Rapids, Michigan: William B. Eerdmans Publishing Company, 1974), page 30.
2. J. Sidlow Baxter, *Explore the Book*, volume 5, (Grand Rapids, Michigan: Zondervan Corporation, 1966), pages 117-125,229.
3. Morris, pages 22-26.
4. I. Howard Marshall, *The Gospel of Luke* (Grand Rapids, Michigan: William B. Eerdmans Publishing Company, 1978), pages 34-35.
5. Marshall, page 43; Morris, pages 66-67.

OUTLINE OF THE GOSPEL OF LUKE

A. Prologue (1:1-4)

B. The infancy stories (1:5-2:52)
    1. John's birth foretold (1:5-25)
    2. Jesus' birth foretold (1:26-38)
    3. Mary visits Elizabeth (1:39-56)
    4. John's birth (1:57-80)
    5. Jesus' birth (2:1-20)
    6. Jesus presented at the Temple (2:21-40)
    7. Jesus at twelve (2:41-52)

C. From John the Baptist to Jesus (3:1-4:13)
    1. The message of John (3:1-20)
    2. The baptism of Jesus (3:21-22)
    3. The genealogy of Jesus (3:23-37)
    4. The temptations of Jesus (4:1-13)

D. Jesus' ministry in Galilee (4:14-9:50)
    1. Jesus at Nazareth (4:14-30)
    2. Healings in Capernaum (4:31-44)
    3. The first disciples called (5:1-11)
    4. A leper cleansed (5:12-16)
    5. A paralytic healed (5:17-26)
    6. Jesus and sinners (5:27-32)
    7. Fasting (5:33-39)
    8. The Sabbath (6:1-11)
    9. The choice of the Twelve (6:12-16)
    10. The sermon on the plain (6:17-49)
    11. A centurion's servant healed (7:1-10)
    12. A woman's son resurrected (7:11-17)
    13. Jesus answers John the Baptist (7:18-23)

TIMELINE FOR LUKE'S GOSPEL

	0AD	30AD	60AD
JESUS AND LUKE	■ Jesus born ca. 6/4 BC	■ Jesus crucified ca. 30 AD	■ *Luke* writes his Gospel ca. 63/72 AD
HIGH PRIESTS	*Annas* 6-15 AD → *Eleazar* 15-18 AD → *Caiaphas* 18-37 AD →		
RULERS IN PALESTINE	*Herod* the Great 37-4 BC → *Herod Antipas* king of Galilee and Perea 4 BC-39 AD (deposed) → *Archilaus* king of Judea 4 BC-6 AD (deposed for brutality) → ■ Emperor puts Judea under direct Roman administration 6 AD	*Pontius Pilate* procurator of Judea 26-36 AD (deposed for maladministration) →	■ First Jewish revolt 66 AD ■ Jerusalem finally destroyed 70 AD
ROMAN EMPERORS	*Augustus Caesar* 29 BC-14 AD →	*Tiberius* 14-37 AD → *Gaius Caligula* 37-41 AD → *Claudius* 41-54 AD → *Nero* 54-68 AD →	

18

PART ONE
GALILEE

LUKE 1:1-4

Overview

The best way to introduce yourself to Luke's Gospel is to read it through, in one sitting if possible. It should take you about two hours if you read quickly for an overall impression. If your Bible includes subtitles for passages, use them as clues to the story's movement. (If you read slowly or are pressed for time, try to take at least half an hour to read sizable portions of the book. Look at the birth section, parts of Jesus' ministry, and the Passion account.)

As you read, jot down answers to questions 1-4 and 8.

First impressions

1. What are your first impressions of Luke's book? (For instance, what is it about? What overall impression does it give you of Jesus?)

_____

_____

_____

_____

_____

_____

_____

For Thought and Discussion: What do you notice about the style of Luke's book? For instance, how is it like and unlike biographies and stories people write today? Is it fun to read? Why or why not?

21

For Further Study:
Look for examples of
the following in Jesus'
teaching and actions:
  ordinary people
  medical interest
  personal details
    (like age)
  signs of emotion

2. Repetition is a clue to the ideas an author
   wants to stress. What key words or phrases does
   Luke (or Jesus) use over and over?

   _____

   _____

   _____

   _____

   _____

   _____

   _____

   _____

3. Look for at least one example of each of the following of Luke's (and Jesus') interests.

   a. poverty

      in Jesus' personal life _manger birth (2:7)_

      _____

      in Jesus' teaching _____

      _____

      _____

      in people Jesus encountered _____

      _____

      _____

   b. women

      people Jesus encountered _____

      _____

      in Jesus' teaching _____

      _____

      _____

c. prayer

　　in Jesus' personal life _____

　　_____

　　in His teaching _____

　　_____

　　in others' lives _____

　　_____

d. the Holy Spirit

　　in Jesus' personal life _____

　　_____

　　in His teaching _____

　　_____

　　in others' lives _____

　　_____

e. salvation for the whole world

　　in Jesus' teaching _____

　　_____

　　_____

　　in words about Jesus _____

　　_____

　　_____

　　in Jesus' actions _____

　　_____

　　_____

4. If you find outlining helpful, fill in the following outline with titles for the various sections. If you prefer, fill in the outline as you complete each lesson of the study. A detailed outline appears on pages 15-17.

1:1-4	Prologue
1:5-4:13	Prelude to ministry

    1:5-2:52 _____

    3:1-20 _____

    3:21-22 _____

    3:23-38 _____

    4:1-13 _____

4:14-9:50   Ministry in Galilee

    4:14-30 _____

    _____

    4:31-5:39 _____

    _____

    6:1-49 _____

    _____

    7:1-50 _____

    _____

    8:1-21 _____

    _____

    8:22-56 _____

    _____

    9:1-50 _____

    _____

9:51-19:44   Travel toward Jerusalem

    9:51-10:24 _____

    _____

Prologue (1:1-4)

In classical Greek style, Luke begins his work with a formal dedication to his patron (the man who is probably helping to pay for publishing the book). The dedication offers several clues to Luke's intent in writing this book.

5. Read 1:1-4 slowly several times, preferably in several translations. What subject does Luke say he is writing about? (Think about what "the things that have been fulfilled [NASB: "accomplished"] among us" are.)

_____

_____

_____

_____

_____

6. What does *Luke say* is his purpose for writing his Gospel (1:3-4)?

_____

_____

_____

_____

_____

7. From questions 1-6 and any other observations you have made, try to summarize in your own words what *you think* is the purpose of Luke's Gospel.

_____

_____

_____

_____

_____

_____

_____

_____

For Thought and Discussion: What is your own purpose for studying Luke's Gospel? How does it compare with 1:4?

Study Skill—Application

The last step of Bible study is asking yourself, "What difference should this passage make to my life? How should it make me want to think or act?" Application will require time, thought, prayer, and perhaps even discussion with another person.

At times, you may find it most productive to concentrate on one specific application, giving it careful thought and prayer. At other times you may want to list many implications a passage of Scripture has for your life, and then choose one to concentrate on for prayer and action. Use whatever method helps you to grow more obedient to God's Word.

Some possible applications for a passage are: "I need to pray about . . . consistently for the next week, asking for ability, guidance, and discipline to obey by God's strength." "I need to stop . . . ." "I need to ask the Holy Spirit to help me . . . ." "I need to do . . . ."

As you plan applications, remember that both you and God have responsibilities for your spiritual growth (Philippians 2:12-13). Because we are dependent upon God, application must be saturated with prayer for guidance, ability, forgiveness, discipline, etc.

27

8. Note here any incidents, teachings, topics, or impressions of Jesus in Luke's Gospel that you want to think about this week.

_____

_____

_____

_____

_____

_____

_____

9. In your first reading of Luke's Gospel or in the background on pages 11-14, you may have come across concepts you'd like clarified or questions you'd like answered. While your thoughts are still fresh, jot down your questions here. You can look for answers as you study further.

_____

_____

_____

_____

_____

_____

For the group

This "For the group" section and the ones in later lessons are intended to suggest ways of structuring your discussions. Feel free to select what suits your group. The main goals of this lesson are to get to know the Gospel of Luke in general and the people with whom you are going to study it.

If you read the whole book through, this may be the most time-consuming lesson in the study. The group leader should warn members to allow several hours for reading the book. If reading the whole book is an impossible demand on someone's time, he or she could probably get a general impression of the Gospel by skimming portions of it for the story line and repeated ideas.

Worship. Some groups like to begin with prayer and/or singing. Some pray only briefly for God's guidance at the beginning, but leave extended prayer until after the study.

Warm-up. The beginning of a new study is a good time to lay a foundation for honest sharing of ideas, for getting comfortable with each other, and for encouraging a sense of common purpose. One way to establish common ground is to talk about what each group member hopes to get out of your group—out of your study of Luke, and out of any prayer, singing, sharing, outreach, or anything else you might do together. You can include what you hope to give to the group as well. If you have someone write down each member's hopes and expectations, then you can look back at these goals later to see if they are being met. You can then plan more time for prayer or decide to cover Luke more slowly if necessary.

You may decide to take about fifteen minutes at the beginning of your discussion of lesson one to discuss goals. Or, you may prefer to take a whole meeting to hand out study guides, introduce the study, examine the "How to Use This Study" section on pages 5-9, and discuss goals.

First impressions. From lesson one you should get, above all, first impressions of the book's themes and purposes on which to build deeper discoveries later. To focus your discussion, each group member might choose one scene or teaching that was especially meaningful to him or her, and explain why. Ask the group to describe Jesus briefly. This open sharing could help introduce members who do not know each other well.

You probably won't need to discuss answers for questions 3 and 4; they are meant to help focus your attention as you read the Gospel for the first time. However, do try to summarize Luke's purpose for writing his book (questions 5-7).

Application. If application is unfamiliar to some group members, choose a sample paragraph from the Gospel and discuss possible ways of applying it. Try to state specifically how the passage is relevant to you and how you might act in light of it. Think of responses that you might actually do, not just ideal responses. Don't neglect that prayer for ability, courage, discipline, and guidance to do something are appropriate applications of a passage.

Give the group a chance to voice any questions about the book or the historical background. You may decide to postpone answering some questions until you deal with the relevant passage, but you can keep the group's questions in mind.

Wrap-up. The wrap-up is a time to bring the discussion to a focused end and to make any announcements about the next lesson or meeting. For example, lesson two covers two long chapters. Look at it ahead of time and decide whether you should cover it in two meetings. At the end of this meeting, let the group know how much of lesson two to prepare for next time.

Worship. Praise God for His wisdom in giving us four Gospels, and especially for the Gospel of Luke. Praise Him for what He reveals about Himself in this book. Ask Him to teach you to know, love, and obey Him through your study of Luke's Gospel.

LUKE 1:5-2:52

Two Babies

In lesson one you thought about the purpose of Luke's Gospel. One simple summary of that purpose is: "To explain the good news about Jesus." For the rest of this study, we will focus on this purpose. We will look for the *content* of the good news and the *response* Luke urges us to make to it. The content is Jesus—His identity, character, mission, and message.

For this lesson, read through all of 1:5-2:52 first. You would benefit from reading it in several different translations. Ask God to enlighten your mind to understand and soften your heart to respond.

Luke's style changes in 1:5. The prologue (1:1-4) is in literary Greek, but the infancy stories use a Hebrew style of speaking.[1] Many of the scenes and customs of Jewish Palestine would have been as foreign to Luke's Greek-Roman audience as they are to us. The ethnic style and exotic setting must have made this tale of angels and miracle births seem even more improbable to a sophisticated man like Theophilus. Perhaps Luke wanted his patron to face squarely the extraordinary way God had chosen to intervene in history.[2]

As you read 1:5-2:52, do the following:

1) Look for important words. Find in a dictionary or note in the study guide's margins any words you do not understand.

2) Get a sense of what the passage is about.

When you have read 1:5-2:52 once, then go back and work on the questions below. Use the

For Further Study:
Verse 17 recalls
Malachi 3:1, 4:5-6.
   a. What do you
think "to turn the
hearts of the fathers
to their children"
means?
   b. Why do you
think turning fathers'
hearts to their chil-
dren is part of prepar-
ing the people for the
Lord to come?

margins and any other blank space to jot thoughts
on the optional questions. If an idea for personal
application strikes you, turn to page 41 and write
your idea under question 14, so that you won't
forget it.

   This lesson covers two long chapters. We didn't
want to separate them because Luke has shaped
them as a unit. However, feel free to take two weeks
for this lesson if you need more time.

John's birth foretold (1:5-25)

Herod (1:5). Herod the Great ruled Judea from 40[3]
   to 4 BC. The events of chapters 1 and 2 took
   place near the end of his reign.

Priestly divisions (1:5). The Aaronic branch of the
   tribe of Levi was divided into twenty-four
   priestly divisions; that of Abijah was the eighth.
   Most priests lived in the countryside of Judea
   and traveled to Jerusalem for a week every six
   months to serve in their division's turn in the
   Temple. Since there were a great many priests,
   duties were assigned *by lot* (1:9).

Your prayer has been heard (1:13). It was customary for the priest who offered the evening sacrifice to pray for the deliverance of Israel from
   oppression. Since Zechariah had won the once-
   in-a-lifetime chance to offer the evening
   incense, he was probably thinking of his priestly
   office rather than his personal desires.[4]

Wine (1:15). A man could vow to abstain from alco-
   holic drinks and from cutting his hair as a special act of dedication to the Lord. Such a man
   was called a "Nazirite" (Numbers 6:1-21). Sam-
   son (Judges 13:4-7) and Samuel (1 Samuel
   1:11) were dedicated as Nazirites from birth.

1. What do you learn from 1:5-25 about each of
   the following:

   John the Baptist's mission (1:15-17) _____

_____

_____

_____

_____

how people should respond (1:14-20) _____

_____

_____

_____

_____

Optional Application: a. Have you ever responded to God's promises as Zechariah did (1:18)? What tempts you to do this, and how can you overcome this temptation?

b. Contrast Zechariah in Luke 1:11-20 with Abraham in Genesis 15:1-6, 17:15-21.

For Thought and Discussion: a. Compare Mary's response in 1:34 to Zechariah's in 1:18. Why did Mary receive no rebuke?

b. How can you cultivate Mary's attitude?

Disgrace (1:25). Barrenness was regarded as divine disfavor. Elizabeth's experience repeated Sarah's (Genesis 16-17,21) and Hannah's (1 Samuel 1-2).

Jesus' birth foretold (1:26-38)

Pledged (1:27). Betrothal was a binding contract breakable only by divorce.

His father David (1:32). God had promised that a descendant of King David would inherit his throne and reign permanently over Israel (2 Samuel 7:13,16; Isaiah 9:6-7). The Jews called this descendant the *Messiah* (Greek: *Christ*), which means "Anointed One."

2. Gabriel said two things about Jesus's identity (1:32-33). Who was Jesus going to be?

a. _____

_____

b. _____

_____

For Further Study:
Notice the repeated
word "joy" in
1:14,44,47,58; 2:10.
What is Luke's point?

**Optional
Application:**
Respond to God's
deeds of salvation for
you as Mary and
Elizabeth did.

Mary visits Elizabeth (1:39-56)

Jewish women commonly spent the first months of
pregnancy isolated from normal duties and people
(see 1:24). Mary may have also needed to escape
neighbors gossiping about an unwed mother.

The hymn in 1:46-55 is known as the Magnificat because its first word in Latin is *Magnificat*,
"glorifies." Luke includes three other hymns in
1:5-2:52.

Some people think that Mary was praising God
for what He did in Old Testament times; others
think she was prophesying what God was beginning
to do through Jesus. Old Testament prophets often
spoke of the future in the past tense (Isaiah 53) to
show the certainty of the prediction.

3. Mary calls God "my Savior" in 1:47. How does
   she portray God as Savior in 1:48-55?

   _____

   _____

   _____

   _____

   _____

   _____

4. What does 1:39-56 reveal about Jesus' identity
   and mission (1:43,51-55)?

   _____

   _____

   _____

   _____

5. How do Mary and Elizabeth respond to this
   revelation?

   _____

   _____

34

_____

_____

John's birth (1:57-80)

━━━━━━━━━━━━━━━━━━━━━━━━━━━━━

**Optional
Application:**
Meditate on true
peace this week.
Thank God for it.

**For Thought and
Discussion:** Com-
pare John's identity
(1:76) to Jesus'
(1:32).

Salvation (1:69). This is one of Luke's favorite
 words; he uses it much more than the other
 Gospel writers. It means deliverance from all
 manner of ills, for the Greek word *soteria* means
 "salvation," "deliverance," and "healing." Perhaps Luke the physician liked to see Jesus' work
 as the ultimate fulfillment of his own calling.

Peace (1:79). See the box, "Peace on Earth" on
 page 43.

Lived in the desert (1:80). John's parents were old
 when he was born and probably died soon after.
 There were several communities of religious
 Jews in the wilderness of Judea between Jerusalem and the Dead Sea.[5]

6. Zechariah's prophecy in Luke 1:68-79 is called
 the Benedictus, Latin for "Praise be." For what
 character qualities and acts does Zechariah
 praise God in 1:68-79?

 redemption from slavery for Israel (1:68).

 _____

 _____

 _____

 _____

7. How does 1:68-79 further reveal . . .

 John's mission? _____

 _____

 _____

Optional Application: a. Does 1:74-75 have any implications for your prayer or priorities? If so, what are they?

b. How is Jesus' mission as Savior of the world relevant to your current situation? Meditate on what it means for Jesus to be Savior—"If Jesus is my Savior, then . . . ."

_____

_____

Jesus' mission (1:78-79)? _____

_____

_____

_____

_____

8. Zechariah said that the Lord would rescue the Jews because of the covenant (pact, treaty) He had made with their ancestors (verses 72-73). What would be the ultimate goal of this deliverance and this covenant (verses 74-75)?

_____

_____

_____

_____

_____

Jesus' birth (2:1-20)

Luke 2:1 puts these events into the context of world history. God used a Roman emperor to fulfill the plan He announced in Micah 5:2. This census probably occurred sometime between 6 and 4 BC.

Joseph and Mary had a three-day trip from Nazareth to Bethlehem. It must have seemed miserable timing to the woman—nine months pregnant and riding a donkey or walking all day in the dust and weather. Possibly not every family had to return to ancestral homes; Joseph may have had property in Bethlehem.[6]

The town of David (2:4). Jerusalem, 4½ miles away, was usually given this title, but David was brought up at Bethlehem.

Manger (2:7). A feeding trough for animals.

Cloth (2:7). Newborn babies were normally wrapped to make them feel secure. The cloths also helped to prevent babies' soft limbs from being distorted.[7]

Shepherds (2:8). They were classed with prostitutes and tax collectors as scum because 1) they could not keep the ceremonial law, which restricted, for example, the touching of dead things; and 2) they traveled around with loose habits, no fixed residence, and few scruples about other people's property. Considered untrustworthy, shepherds were forbidden to testify in court.

Despite this stereotype, however, these shepherds may have already been devout or ready to hear the good news. It is significant that God chose to announce His Son's birth to real shepherds rather than to the religious and civil leaders, who were supposed to be His people's shepherds longing for the Messiah (Ezekiel 34:1-31).[8]

Men on whom his favor rests (2:14). "Favor" is extraordinary kindness, grace. (See 1:28,30). RSV translates "peace among men with whom he is pleased," and KJV reads "peace, good will toward men."

For Thought and Discussion: What was God saying by having His Son's birth announced to such people as shepherds, rather than to the nation's official shepherds (leaders) or at least to people considered respectable? Are Luke 5:32; 6:20,24; 11:46-52 relevant?

For Thought and Discussion: What did the angels mean by proclaiming peace to those whom God favored?

For Thought and Discussion: a. To whom does God assure peace in 2:14? Why to them? (Consider Proverbs 16:7.)

b. Trace the idea of God's pleasure in 3:2, 10:21, 12:32.

9. Why did God have His Son born in the circumstances described in 2:7, rather than in a royal or at least comfortable household? (See Luke 6:20, 9:58, 22:27; 2 Corinthians 8:9.)

_____

_____

_____

_____

_____

_____

_____

For Further Study:
Compare 2:10-14 to
Isaiah 9:6.

**Optional
Application:** The Son
of God was born in a
stable. What implica-
tions does this fact
have for the way you
view your own situa-
tion? Talk to God
about this.

10. What does 2:1-20 reveal about . . .

Jesus' identity (2:11)? _____

_____

_____

_____

_____

how people and angels respond to His coming
(2:14-20)?

_____

_____

_____

_____

Jesus presented in the Temple (2:21-40)

Purification (2:22). A mother was ritually unclean
for forty days after bearing a son; on the fortieth
day she brought a sacrifice to the Temple (Leviticus 12:1-8). Contact with symbols of life and
death—corpses, semen, menstrual blood,
birthing—demanded separation from holy
(divine, immortal) things (Leviticus 15). Joseph
and Jesus were probably also unclean from having touched Mary. Mary's sacrifice (Luke 2:24)
was the smallest permitted, that of a poor
person.
   This utter separation between the Creator
who is eternal spirit and creatures that are born
physically was deeply ingrained in the Jews. The
belief that the Holy Lord had become a human
woman's baby was blasphemous to most Jews.

Present him (2:22). Every firstborn belonged to
God; he had to be either ransomed with a fee or
offered to God (Exodus 13:2,12-13). If offered,
he crossed the barrier between the common and
the holy (1 Samuel 1:11,22,28). Jesus was

evidently offered to become holy, set apart for God's service.

11. What do you learn from 2:21-40 about . . .

Jesus' mission (2:30-35)? _____

_____

_____

_____

_____

how people respond to Him (2:28,38)? _____

_____

_____

_____

_____

For Further Study: The teachers with whom Jesus talked in the Temple (2:46) were rabbis discussing interpretations of the Law and the Prophets (two of the three main sections of the Old Testament). What attitude toward the Law did Jesus show in this episode?

For Thought and Discussion: How is Jesus a model for Christian children in 2:40,49,51?

Jesus at twelve (2:41-52)

The Law commanded adult males to attend three feasts each year: Passover, Pentecost (Weeks), and Tabernacles (Booths). (See Exodus 23:14-17, Deuteronomy 16:16.) Distance hindered many people, but most tried to be in Jerusalem for Passover.

At twelve, Jesus had one more year until He would be considered an adult responsible for keeping the Law. On this trip He would have been preparing to participate in the ceremonies the next year.

Jews normally referred to God as "Our Father" or "Our Father in heaven." As early as twelve, Jesus passed over this formal address to say "my Father" (Luke 2:49), a child's familiar term for his daddy (compare 11:2).

12. What does 2:40-52 reveal about . . .

Jesus' identity (2:49)? _____

_____

39

For Further Study:
What do you learn about the Holy Spirit from the following verses:
1:15,35,41,67;
2:25,27?

For Further Study:
Luke tried to show in his Gospel that everything in history happens according to God's plan. How do chapters 1 and 2 reflect this theme? (See, for instance, 2:1-3.)

Jesus' character (2:40,43-47,49,51-52)? _____

_____

_____

_____

_____

_____

Summary and response

> **Study Skill—Summarizing the Passage**
> A good way to see whether you have understood a passage of Scripture is to try summarizing it in your own words. When the passage tells a story like Luke 1:5-2:52, it can be helpful to write not just what happened, but also what the events have to do with the main themes and purposes of the book.

13. a. What does Luke say about the *content* of the good news in 1:5-2:52? (See 1:11-17,26-35, 50-55,68-79; 2:11,14,30-32,34-35.)

_____

_____

_____

_____

_____

_____

_____

40

b. Summarize the *response* people make to the good news in these chapters. (See 1:18,38, 42-47,67-68; 2:17,20,28,38.)

_____

_____

_____

_____

_____

Optional Application: From the prophecies in chapters 1 and 2, describe at least one way in which Jesus' coming affects you— your life, your needs, your present, your future, your relationships.

14. Reread the box on application on page 27. Then prayerfully consider whether anything in 1:5-2:52 has implications for your life today. Think about the Optional Applications in this lesson, as well as anything else that impressed you.

   a. What one insight from this lesson would you like to focus on for application this week?

   _____

   _____

   _____

   _____

   b. Write down at least one way in which this insight is relevant to your actions toward God, other people, or circumstances.

   _____

   _____

   _____

   _____

   _____

   c. What one concrete step can you take (consistent prayer, a decision, a change of attitude toward circumstances, action, etc.) in light of this insight?

   _____

Optional Application: Think about the responses people made to the good news. Do any of them suggest ways you might respond to 1:5-2:52? What practical steps could you take to follow the examples of the people Luke describes?

15. List any questions you have about anything in this lesson.

For the group

Worship.

Warm-up. A simple question that deals generally with the topic of the study but focuses on people's experience can help the group shift from the day's affairs to Bible study. You needn't even discuss the warm-up question; you can just think about it for a moment. A possible warm-up for this lesson is, "What is the message of Christmas?"

Read aloud. Even when the group has studied the passage ahead of time, most people will be glad to have their memories refreshed. So, read through all of 1:5-2:52 before beginning to discuss. It will be more interesting if you have a different person read each scene.

Summarize. A quick summary at the outset helps to set a context for the rest of the discussion. Briefly, what is 1:5-2:52 about? Don't expect as rich a summary now as you will get at the end of your discussion, but do give the group a chance to observe the forest before you start analyzing trees.

Two Babies. It can be dull to go through a lesson asking, "What did you get for number one? . . . two? . . ." To avoid repetition and help people organize their thoughts, you can center your discussion around the book's themes, like this:

42

1. What do 1:5-25 and 1:57-80 tell you about John's mission (questions 1, 7)?
2. What can we learn about Jesus' identity from the various scenes in chapters 1 and 2 (questions 2, 4, 10, 12)?
3. What do these chapters reveal about Jesus' mission (questions 2, 4, 7, 11)?
4. What character traits does Jesus show in 2:40-52 (question 12)?
5. How do various people respond to the good news?
6. How is Jesus' identity and mission relevant to you? How do you think Luke wants his readers, Theophilus and you, to respond to these chapters? How can you respond this week? How can you respond as a group to the news announced in chapters 1 and 2?

Summarize. Summarize the content of the gospel and the responses you've observed in 1:5-2:52. Then summarize the kinds of applications you plan to make.

Wrap-up. Lesson three begins to cover Luke's Gospel more slowly, so you should have more time to discuss personal applications. You could plan five or ten minutes at the beginning of your next meeting to share any insights or questions about this lesson's applications. Don't let the group get the impression that everyone must report some measurable change in his life; just allow time to share what the group is thinking.

Worship. Thank God for sending His Son Jesus as the fulfillment of His promises to the Jews. Meditate together on Jesus' identity as Son of God and His mission as Savior of the world. The four hymns in 1:5-2:52 can be guidelines for your praise.

Peace on Earth

The Roman emperor Caesar Augustus (Luke 2:1) brought the *Pax Romana* ("Roman Peace") to the Mediterranean world in 27 BC. The Roman Peace meant that the Empire's people were secure from invasion and safe to travel and trade freely.

(continued on page 44)

(continued from page 43)

However, to the people of Judea there was no peace as long as Roman soldiers occupied their land and Roman tax collectors took their money. The Jews hoped for a Messiah who would liberate them politically and make them a strong nation (Isaiah 9:2-7, 11:4; Luke 1:68-74)—this was their idea of the "Prince of Peace" (Isaiah 9:6).

But "peace" meant much more than political security to the Old Testament prophets. The Jews were correct in believing that the Roman Peace was no true peace, but they were wrong in reading prophecies selectively. The promised "peace" of the Messiah meant wholeness and wellness in all of creation—reconciliation between God and man, psychological rest and health, physical wholeness, social harmony, abundant harvest, and also political security. All the latter aspects of peace would grow from the former; God would end the enmity between Himself and man, and His presence would heal all other hurts.[9]

1. Morris, page 26; Marshall, page 46.
2. Michael Wilcock, *Savior of the World: The Message of Luke's Gospel* (Downers Grove, Illinois: InterVarsity Press, 1979), pages 39-40.
3. The beginning of Herod's reign is given as 37 BC in *The NIV Study Bible*, page 1535; and Henry E. Dosker, "Herod," *The International Standard Bible Encyclopedia*, volume 3, edited by James Orr (Grand Rapids, Michigan: William B. Eerdmans Publishing Company, 1956), page 1379. The date is 40 BC according to Marshall, page 51; and R. E. Nixon, "Matthew," *The New Bible Commentary: Revised*, edited by Donald Guthrie, et al. (Grand Rapids: William B. Eerdmans Publishing Company, 1970), page 818.
4. Morris, page 69.
5. *The NIV Study Bible*, page 1538.
6. Marshall, pages 101-105.
7. W. H. Van Doren, *The Gospel of Luke* (Grand Rapids, Michigan: Kregel Publications, 1981), page 50.
8. Morris, page 84.
9. Hartmut Beck and Colin Brown, "Peace," *The New International Dictionary of New Testament Theology*, volume 2, edited by Colin Brown (Grand Rapids, Michigan: Zondervan Corporation, 1976), pages 776-783.

LUKE 3:1-4:13

From John to Jesus

Luke's Gospel is no biography; in an instant we leap twenty years, and the children of 1:1-2:52 are grown men. The cousins—Son and prophet of the Most High (1:32,76)—meet for perhaps the first time since the womb (1:41).

Before beginning the questions, read all of 3:1-4:13, thinking about the content and response of the good news and the purpose of Luke's book. Then skim all the questions in the lesson before you start to answer any. This preparation will help refresh your memory of the whole passage and will show you where the lesson is going.

John's message (3:1-20)

Luke 3:1-2 dates the beginning of John's ministry. The verses set the story in the context of the political history which God had prepared for the advent of His Son. (See the timeline on page 18.)

Tiberias (3:1). Scholars disagree over when his reign began. His fifteenth year was sometime between 25 and 29 AD. Marshall favors about 28 AD; *The NIV Study Bible* prefers 25-26 AD.[1]

Herod (3:1). Herod the Great was king when Jesus and John were born (1:5); his son Herod Antipas and two other sons succeeded him in 4 BC.

45

For Further Study:
Repentance (3:3) is
literally a "turning
around." Using a dic-
tionary if necessary,
explain what it means
to repent of sin.

Herod Antipas is the Herod in 3:1 and the rest
of the Gospel. He ruled Galilee and Perea from
4 BC to 39 AD.

Tetrarch (3:1). Officially, Herod was a "tetrarch,"
the ruler of one-fourth of Palestine. Ordinary
people in Galilee and Rome called him "king"
(Matthew 14:1, Mark 6:14).[2]

Annas . . . Caiaphas (3:2). Officially, there was only
one high priest at a time. However, the issue
had been confused ever since Rome began to
appoint high priests to assure their loyalty.
Annas was high priest from 6 to 15 AD, when
the emperor replaced him with his son Eleazar.
Another son, Caiaphas, was appointed high
priest from 18 to 37 AD. However, "Jews
regarded the high priesthood as a life-office"
whatever Rome did, so they still considered
Annas to be the real high priest. John 18:13-24
shows that Annas retained "considerable power
behind the scenes."[3]

1. Luke gives a vivid sense of John's character
through dialogue. What did John tell the people
to do?

Luke 3:3 _____

_____

_____

3:8 _____

_____

_____

Baptism (3:3). John's baptism was a new application
of a familiar practice. Jews baptized converts
because they regarded all Gentiles as needing to
be cleansed from sin. John shocked people by
claiming that even Jews needed to be cleansed.

Prepare the way (3:4). In ancient times, a herald
would travel ahead of a royal procession,

announcing the king's coming and command-
ing preparations.

2. What reasons did John give for the instructions
   you listed in question 1?

   3:3 _____

   _____

   _____

   3:4-6 _____

   _____

   _____

   3:7,9 _____

   _____

   _____

**Optional
Application:** Repent-
ance includes atti-
tudes as well as prac-
tices. Consider the
attitude John con-
demned in verse 8.
How might a Christian
be tempted to have a
similar wrong
attitude?

Tax collectors (3:12). These men were hated both as
collaborators (they collected for the hated
Roman occupiers) and as extortioners (Rome
hired them to collect a fixed amount, and any
percentage more than this that they could
extract was their profit).

Soldiers (3:14) These were also privileged, powerful,
and disliked.

3. a. John did not tell tax collectors or soldiers to
      change jobs, but he did tell them how to
      "produce fruit in keeping with repentance."
      What did he say (3:12-14)?

      _____

      _____

      _____

      _____

      _____

For Thought and Discussion: How would the actions John urged help a person to "Prepare the way for the Lord"?

For Further Study: What did John say about the Holy Spirit (3:16-17)?

Optional Application: Does question 5 suggest any action or change of attitude you need to make?

b. Does 3:12-14 offer us a general principle for business conduct, for behavior in the workplace? If so, what is it?

_____

_____

_____

_____

_____

4. John told tax collectors and soldiers to act with *justice* at work. However, what standard did John tell the crowd to apply in their private lives as fruit of repentance (3:11)?

_____

_____

_____

_____

_____

5. Write down one way in which the standard of 3:11 applies to your life and one way in which the business ethic of 3:12-14 applies.

private standard _____

_____

_____

_____

_____

business ethic _____

_____

_____

48

6. Summarize what John prophesied about the "one" who was coming (verses 16-17).

_____

_____

_____

_____

_____

For Further Study: Compare Luke 3:16-17 to Acts 2:1-41 and 1 Corinthians 3:13.

Optional Application: What implications does 3:16-17 have for your conduct?

7. In what way was John's message "good news" (3:18)?

_____

_____

_____

_____

_____

For Thought and Discussion: Does your answer to question 7 motivate you to act on John's message? Why or why not?

8. Does any insight from 3:1-20 suggest a course of action you want to take or a matter you want to pray about? If so, describe what you plan to do.

_____

_____

_____

_____

Jesus' baptism (3:21-22)

9. Jesus' baptism was important for many reasons. What did the Father publicly declare about Jesus at His baptism (3:22)?

_____

_____

_____

For Thought and Discussion: Jesus had never rebelled against the Father's will for His life (Luke 22:42, John 15:10), so He did not need to be baptized for repentance. Why then was Jesus baptized (Matthew 3:14-15, John 1:31-34, 2 Corinthians 5:21, Hebrews 2:17)?

For Further Study: At what other occasions did the Father speak from heaven about Jesus (Luke 9:35, John 12:28)?

10. What did the Holy Spirit do (3:22)?

_____

_____

_____

Jesus' genealogy (3:23-38)

Matthew begins his Gospel with Jesus' genealogy traced down from Abraham through David and Joseph. Jesus was Joseph's legal son in Jewish eyes, even though Joseph was not the natural father. Matthew's purpose is to show the Jews that Jesus is the legal heir of David's kingship and Abraham's covenant.

By contrast, Luke is less concerned to prove to his Gentile audience that Jesus is the King of Israel. Luke traces Jesus' inheritance back through Joseph (His legal father), Heli (Mary's father—Joseph's father-in-law and so his adopted father by Jewish law; compare Luke 3:23-31 to Matthew 1:12-16), David, Abraham, Adam, and God. By following Jesus' biological line, Luke stresses two key facts: Jesus is truly son of Adam, fully human; and Jesus is truly Son of God, the only son of Adam who retains the image of God unmarred by the Fall.

At His baptism, the sinless son of Adam identified with all other men who need God's cleansing, and He was acclaimed Son of God, the Father's only pleasing son. Now Luke inserts a genealogy to show that Jesus was fully son of Adam and Son of God long before that acclamation.

Jesus' temptations (4:1-13)

Immediately after identifying with man in baptism, Jesus goes into the wilderness to be tempted as a man. Having been declared Son of God and filled with the Holy Spirit (3:22, 4:1), Jesus is tempted concerning His submission to the Father and the Spirit.

The Old Testament passages Jesus quotes are from Deuteronomy 8:3 and 6:13,16. This section of Deuteronomy discusses Israel's time of being tested

50

by God in the wilderness. Israel largely failed the test of utter loyalty to God (Deuteronomy 6:4-5, 9:7; Jeremiah 31:31-32). God tested Israel, but the Devil tempts Jesus with the Holy Spirit's permission.

Test (4:12). To make someone prove his love, faithfulness, or ability. See Exodus 17:1-4.

---

11. One purpose of Jesus' baptism was that He might identify fully with man. How did His temptation fulfill a similar purpose (Hebrews 2:18, 4:15)?

_____

_____

_____

_____

_____

12. a. In all three temptations, Satan intended to entice Jesus to grasp by His own power what the Father planned to give in His own time (Philippians 2:6-9). In what specific area was Jesus asked to disobey His Father in each of the three temptations?

4:3-4 _____

_____

_____

4:5-8 _____

_____

4:9-12 _____

_____

_____

For Thought and Discussion: It is right for God to test man to prove his faithfulness, as God tested Israel and Jesus. But it is not right for man to test God (Luke 4:12). Why is this so?

For Thought and Discussion: a. At Jesus' baptism, the Father acknowledged Jesus' birthright as Son of God (1:35; 3:22,38). How was this Sonship connected with Satan's intent in tempting Jesus (4:3,9)?
b. Why did Satan want Jesus to use His supernatural power (4:3,9-11)?

For Thought and Discussion: What conclusions about temptation in our own lives can we draw from the facts that Jesus was tempted by the Devil . . .

a. while He was being led by the Spirit (4:1-2)?

b. while He was fasting and praying in preparation for His ministry (4:14-15)?

Optional Application: Using a topical Bible or concordance, search the Scriptures for passages (such as 1 Corinthians 10:13) that could strengthen you in the temptation that you are currently experiencing.

b. Are you tempted to grasp at anything that God would give by grace in His own time? Or, are you facing some other temptation? Ask God to show you one particular area of temptation, and then describe it.

_____

_____

_____

_____

13. a. What equipment did Jesus use to defend Himself against temptation (4:1,4,8,12)?

_____

_____

_____

_____

b. Did the Son of God use any weapons against temptation that are not available to us? What are the implications of this fact for us?

_____

_____

_____

_____

_____

14. How could you apply Jesus' weapons against the temptation you described in question 12b?

_____

_____

_____

_____

_____

15. a. In summary, what does 3:1-4:13 reveal about the content of the good news (John's message and Jesus' identity, mission, and character)? See 3:3-6,22,38; 4:4,8,12.

_____

_____

_____

_____

_____

b. How would you summarize the way this section encourages us to respond to the good news? See 3:8,11-14; 4:4,8,12.

_____

_____

_____

_____

_____

Study Skill—Outlining the Purpose

An ordinary outline of Luke's Gospel such as the one on pages 15-17 can help you find particular passages, but it tells you little of how the parts fit into Luke's overall message. One way to recall Luke's message at a glance is to outline the way each passage unfolds that message.

For instance, Luke's purpose is to set forth the good news about Jesus in an orderly manner, so that the reader can respond to that news. A broad outline of the book that takes account of this purpose might begin like this:

1:1-4   Prologue: Luke states the purpose of his book.

(continued on page 54)

53

(continued from page 53)

1:5-2:52 Infancy: The Savior and His herald are born miraculously into our world, announced by angels and prophets. The Son of God becomes a Son of Adam.

3:1-4:13 The Savior's herald introduces the good news about repentance and forgiveness. The Savior is declared Son of God and undergoes baptism and temptation as Son of Man—all in preparation to begin His mission.

Get a sheet of paper and begin your own outline of Luke's Gospel that reflects his purpose and themes. You can make up your own summaries for 1:1-4:13 or copy these and begin your own outline with 4:14-44. Try to add a new entry as you complete each lesson.

16. List any questions you have about 3:1-4:13.

_____

_____

_____

_____

For the group

Worship.

Experiences from the last lesson's applications. Ask, "What happened this week after you committed yourselves to apply some insight from Luke 1:5-2:52?" You may hear silence and detect embarrassment, especially if the group is unused to applying what they have learned. Encourage the group to share questions to be discussed and prayed about.

Warm-up. Ask everyone to remember a temptation or testing that he or she experienced during the past few days. Then ask, "How did you deal with that temptation?" Let a few people respond, or let everyone think silently for a minute or two.

Read aloud. Read 3:1-22 and 4:1-13. Instead of reading the genealogy, summarize what point it is meant to make.

Summarize. Briefly, what happens in 3:1-4:13? Why are these events important to the gospel story?

John's message. Questions 1 and 2 ask what John *says*. Ask group members to put this into their own words. Paraphrasing can help you think through the meaning of John's words.

If question 3 seems hard, compare Paul's definition of justice in Romans 13:7—"Give everyone what you owe him." Once the group sees John's basic principle of justice (take only what you are owed), discuss how it applies to you. How are you tempted to take more than you deserve in your work?

John commands justice in professional life, but in private life he commands love—generous self-sacrifice that goes beyond what you owe someone. Paul makes a similar point in Romans 13:8-10. How could group members put John's description of self-sacrifice (Luke 3:11) into practice?

The meanings of baptism with the Holy Spirit and fire and of the burning of the chaff (Luke 3:16-17) are debated. Acts 2:1-41 and 1 Corinthians 3:13 may help your group interpret these things.

Jesus' baptism. This event is important for several reasons:

1. Jesus was consecrated (set apart) for ministry.
2. The Father and the Spirit officially approved Jesus to fulfill His mission. God declared that Jesus met His righteous requirements to be the Savior of the world.
3. John the Baptist announced the arrival of the Messiah and the beginning of His ministry (John 1:29-34).
4. Jesus identified with man's need to be cleansed from sin (2 Corinthians 5:21).
5. Jesus set an example of baptism for His followers.[4]

Jesus' temptation. In this incident, Jesus both fulfills another crucial step on the way to fulfilling His mission and gives us an example for dealing with temptation. Try to give attention to both aspects— Jesus revealing Himself to us and Jesus setting an example for us.

People may be reluctant to disclose their areas of temptation. If you can't get anyone to confess theirs, ask the group to invent a hypothetical temptation that is like jumping off the Temple or bowing down to Satan to gain power. Then invite the group to find passages of Scripture that speak to this matter. Encourage each person to choose some passage to meditate on during the coming week, a passage that will be of use when temptation arises. Or, urge the group to meditate on something in Luke 3:1-4:13.

Summarize. Summarize what you've learned about Jesus, the gospel, and how to live in light of it. Summarize your plans for application also.

Wrap-up.

Worship. Thank God for providing Scripture as a way of escape from your temptations. Ask the Holy Spirit to empower you to recall and draw upon Scripture when you need it. Thank Jesus for entering into your need to be baptized and to fight temptation, so that you would have a model to follow.

1. Marshall, page 133; *The NIV Study Bible*, page 1540-1541.
2. *The NIV Study Bible*, page 1463.
3. Marshall, page 134.
4. *The NIV Study Bible*, page 1446.

LUKE 4:14-44

The Galilean Ministry Begins

Baptized in water, filled with the Holy Spirit, and armed with God's Word against temptations, Jesus is ready to begin His ministry. In 4:14-44 we see Him proclaiming His message by word and deed. Read the whole passage before examining each scene in detail. Pray that God will reveal His Son to you as you study.

At Nazareth (4:14-30)

Between the temptation's end in 4:13 and the events at Nazareth in 4:16-30 lay months of preaching and healing throughout Galilee. The Apostle John records some of that time (John 1:29-2:11 or 1:29-4:42), and Matthew points out that Jesus began His ministry in Capernaum (Matthew 4:12-17). Luke knew that much ministry preceeded the sermon at Nazareth (Luke 4:14-15,23), but he put the Nazareth incident at the head of his story as a symbol of the nation's rejection of Jesus, as a shadow of events to come.[1]

Luke 4:16-30 "is the oldest known account of a synagogue service."[2] The service probably began with prayer. Then followed a reading from the Law (the Teaching of Moses, the first five books of the Bible), and probably a discussion or interpretation of it by the reader. There was no ordained minister; the "ruler of the synagogue" (Luke 8:41) was an elder who invited other laymen to read from and speak on the Scripture. Distinguished visitors often

**Optional
Application:** In what
ways are you in need
of the ministry Jesus
announced in
4:18-19? Ask Him to
do these things in
your life.

received this honor. Since Jesus returned to Nazareth as a local boy who had made a name for Himself
in a nearby town (Luke 4:14-15), it was fitting that
He should be invited to give the Sabbath address.

After the Law came a reading from the
Prophets. There was probably no fixed schedule of
prophetic readings at this time,[3] as there was for the
Law. The ruler may have selected the prophetic passage, or he may have left Jesus full or partial freedom to choose His text. In Nazareth He read Isaiah
61:1-2. This section of Isaiah includes several passages about the "Servant of the Lord" who would
save Israel.

1. Summarize the message Jesus announced in
   4:18-21.

   _____

   _____

   _____

   _____

   _____

   _____

The year of the Lord's favor (4:19). Leviticus
   25:8-55 required that every fifty years slaves had
   to be freed, debts canceled, and property
   returned to its ancestral owners. This law of the
   Year of Jubilee was seldom observed (Jeremiah
   34:8-16), but for the prophets and later Jews it
   represented the time of God's great liberation,
   the Messianic Age.

Sat down (Luke 4:20). "It was customary to stand
   while reading Scripture (4:16) but to sit while
   teaching."[4]

2. In what sense was Isaiah 61:1-2 "fulfilled" in
   the hearing of Jesus' audience (Luke 4:21)?

   _____

_____

_____

_____

_____

Optional Application: Have you ever expected Jesus to do for you what you have heard He has done for other people, as the Nazarenes did (4:23)? How can you adopt a right attitude toward His promises in 4:18-19? Ask God to make you like Jesus in this area.

3. a. Jesus' former neighbors were at first so impressed with His wisdom—"Isn't this Joseph's son?" they asked delightedly (4:22).[5] But whose son was He (1:35; 3:22,23,38; 4:3)?

_____

_____

b. Why was the Nazarenes' error crucial in light of the proclamation in 4:18-21?

_____

_____

_____

_____

_____

Physician, heal yourself (4:23). We might say, "Charity begins at home." The supposed son of Joseph had been performing healings in Capernaum for months, and the Nazarenes felt they deserved some benefit from one of their own.

Elijah . . . Elisha (4:25-27). When God afflicted Israel for worshiping Baal, Elijah spent the drought not with a good Jewish widow but with a Phoenician widow near Sidon (1 Kings 16:29-17:24). Later, Elisha healed none of the lepers in Israel, but only Israel's arch-enemy, the Syrian military commander Naaman (2 Kings 5:1-27).

4. Jesus deliberately reminded the Nazarenes that He had been healing other people and that God had frequently blessed the scorned Gentiles.

59

Optional Application: How can you acquire the peace in the face of threat that Jesus shows in 4:30? Consider meditating on God's promises and your relationship to Him.

a. What wrong attitudes did Jesus expose in His people (Luke 4:23-28)?

_____

_____

_____

_____

b. What did He want them—and us—to understand about God and His Kingdom?

_____

_____

_____

_____

5. How would you describe Jesus' character from 4:14-30 (especially 4:21,23-27,30)?

_____

_____

_____

_____

_____

Study Skill—Five Questions

The following five questions may aid you in applying God's Word. When you study a passage, try asking yourself:

Is there a *sin* for me to avoid?
Is there a *promise* for me to trust?
Is there an *example* for me to follow?
Is there a *command* for me to obey?
How can this passage increase my *knowledge* of the Lord (not just knowledge about Him)?

You can recall these five questions by remembering the acronym SPECK—Sin, Promise, Example, Command, Knowledge.

6. a. Is there a sin, promise, etc. in 4:14-30 that you would like to apply to your own life? If so, what is it?

_____

_____

_____

_____

_____

   b. Through what prayer and/or action can you cooperate with God as He transforms you in this area?

_____

_____

_____

_____

_____

At Capernaum (4:31-44)

After His rejection in Nazareth, Jesus returned to Capernaum, where He had been living for some time (Matthew 4:13). This fishing village on the shore of the Sea of Galilee was a good central place for a home base. From there Jesus would take trips around Galilee, teaching in synagogues and the open countryside.

7. Observe all that Jesus did at Capernaum (4:31-41). What did His spoken word accomplish in 4:32,35,39?

_____

_____

_____

_____

_____

61

For Thought and Discussion: According to Luke 11:20, what did Jesus' authority over demons prove?

8. Why were people amazed at Jesus' teaching (4:32; compare Mark 1:22)?

_____

_____

_____

_____

_____

Authority and power (4:36). The Galileans had seen other traveling wonderworkers cast out demons; this was a rare but not unique talent. However, most exorcists required a long process of invoking power, arguing with the demon, extracting its name, and so on. By contrast, Jesus cut short the battle of will and issued a simple command (4:35).

9. What authority gave Jesus the power simply to command evil spirits (11:20)?

_____

_____

_____

_____

When the sun was setting (4:40). According to Jewish tradition, it was unlawful on the Sabbath to carry a burden, travel more than two-thirds of a mile, or heal someone whose life was not in immediate danger. Therefore, the people had to wait until after sunset, when the Sabbath ended.

10. Compare Jesus' word of preaching in 4:18-21 to His word of power in 4:31-41. How were teaching and action related?

_____

_____

_____

_____

_____

Optional Application: Tell someone the good news about Jesus that you've studied in 4:14-44.

Optional Application: Reflect on the connection between Jesus' peace (4:30), authority (4:32,36), and prayer (4:42). Ask God how you could more fully follow Jesus' example in this matter. Spend some time with Him.

The kingdom of God (4:43). This phrase occurs more than thirty times in Luke's Gospel. It has many meanings, including: "the eternal kingship of God; the presence of the kingdom in the person of Jesus, the King; the approaching spiritual form of the kingdom; the future kingdom."[6] In other words, the Kingdom of God "is the rule of God and is both a present reality and a future hope."[7] Watch for this phrase in Jesus' teaching.

11. Jesus said His ministry was to "preach the good news [*euangelizesthai*] of the kingdom of God" (4:43). What have you learned about the Kingdom from 4:14-41?

_____

_____

_____

_____

_____

_____

_____

12. a. After healing all night, what did Jesus do (Luke 4:42, 5:16; Mark 1:35)?

_____

_____

63

Optional Application: Jesus has made His authority available to us (John 14:12-14). What steps could you take to participate in His ministry as 4:18-19,32 describes it?

For Further Study: Reread the Study Skill on pages 53-54. Then add to your own outline a summary of 4:14-44 that shows how the passage fits into Luke's unfolding story of the gospel.

b. Why did He need to do this?

_____

_____

_____

_____

_____

13. If anything else in 4:14-44 prompts you to a specific response, write down what it is and how you intend to respond.

_____

_____

_____

_____

_____

14. List any questions you have about 4:14-44.

_____

_____

_____

_____

For the group

The focus of this lesson is how Jesus began to proclaim His message by word and deed. Draw attention to the way each supported the other—explanation and demonstration.

Worship.

Warm-up. Ask the group to think about this question: "In what one aspect of your life—physical, emotional, mental, relational, spiritual—would you most like God to bring healing or freedom?"

Remember that healing, freedom, and safety are all aspects of salvation.

Read aloud.

Summarize.

At Nazareth. You will notice Luke's themes again in questions 1-5: Jesus' message (question 1), His mission (2), people's response (3a), the message (3b), Jesus' character (5). Question 6 offers each person a chance to apply something of this to himself or herself. You can discuss one or two of the Optional Applications, or you can let each person respond to question 6.

It isn't necessary for everyone to have a specific plan of action for each application question. Most people are able to give attention to only one application at a time. If someone still wants to pray and think about something he or she learned in lesson three, then he or she may not make a specific application from lesson four. Explain to the group that active applications are necessary, but a new one each week is not a rule. Also, explain that application sometimes means activity and sometimes fervent, persistent prayer.

At Capernaum.

Summarize.

Wrap-up.

Worship. Praise God for the compassion, the faithfulness, and the power He reveals in 4:14-44. Thank Him for the works of healing and liberation you see Him doing. Spend time with Him, as Jesus did to gain strength and peace for His ministry. Ask God to enable you to enter more fully into the task of proclaiming the good news of the Kingdom.

1. Wilcock, pages 60-61.
2. Marshall, page 181.
3. Morris, page 106.
4. *The NIV Study Bible*, page 1545.
5. Wilcock, page 61.
6. *The NIV Study Bible*, page 1546.
7. *The NIV Study Bible*, page 1444.

LUKE 5:1-32

Confrontations

The people in Nazareth were typical of the nation. They expected the son of Joseph; they got the Son of God. They wanted Him to satisfy their hopes; they rejected Him when He exposed their beliefs as contrary to God's character.

Jesus continued to make enemies of people who wanted to be righteous by their own standards, but He made disciples of those who would accept His standards. As you read 5:1-32, observe the effects of Jesus' word of authority.

The first disciples called (5:1-11)

Lake of Gennesaret (5:1). The Sea of Galilee. Simon Peter lived in Capernaum, a fishing town on the shore of the lake.

Study Skill—Observing and Interpreting
To study a scene in a Gospel, begin by noticing every detail, even the seemingly trivial—there was a lake called Gennesaret; Jesus spoke to crowds; etc. From these observations, decide which are the key words in the scene. Ask yourself questions about these words—who, what, when, where, how, and why.

1. Simon had known Jesus for some time. He knew that John the Baptist had called Jesus "the Lamb of God" (John 1:35-42) and that Jesus had healed his mother-in-law (Luke 4:38-39).

   Does Luke 5:3 suggest that Simon acknowledged Jesus' authority as a religious teacher? How can you tell?

   _____

   _____

   _____

   _____

All night (5:5). That was the normal time for deep-sea fishing.[1] Simon knew that fishing during the day would be useless.

---

2. Simon knew that Jesus was no fisherman, but he had enough respect for the teacher not to scoff when Jesus suggested fishing at an absurd time (5:4-5). How did Jesus prove to Simon that He had authority over more than religious things (5:6-10)?

   _____

   _____

   _____

   _____

3. a. How did Jesus' demonstration of authority over fish affect Simon (5:8)?

   _____

   _____

   _____

   _____

b. Why do you think authority over fish had this affect on the fisherman, an effect that religious authority alone did not have?

_____

_____

_____

_____

_____

Optional Application: a. Have you ever seen Jesus' authority over all of life as Simon did? If so, how did the experience affect you?

b. Meditate this week on Jesus' authority and the response He asks of you. How could you act on 5:10-11?

4. Jesus used this incident to bring Simon, James, and John from mere interested followers to convicted disciples (5:8,10-11). What can we learn about how discipleship happens from 5:1-11?

_____

_____

_____

_____

_____

_____

5. a. Is there any insight from 5:1-11 that you would like to meditate on and apply this week? If so, what is that truth?

_____

_____

_____

_____

b. How can you act on this truth?

_____

_____

_____

_____

69

Optional Application: a. Have you ever needed to be touched as the leper was? If so, how can you respond to Jesus for doing this? How can you bear a public testimony to your cure?

b. How can you follow Jesus' example in 5:13 and "touch" a "leper" you encounter?

Optional Application: If you feel you need it, ask Jesus to touch you as He touched the leper. Ask in confidence that He is willing to do this.

A leper cleansed (5:12-16)

Leprosy (5:12). In biblical times, this included several skin diseases, such as skin cancers, herpes, and the illness we call leprosy. Some of the diseases were hideous to see and smell, but all lepers were quarantined and survived only on charity. Their sickness was considered punishment for sin, and it barred them from human contact and religious worship. Anyone who touched a leper was thereby unclean and so had to avoid people and worship for a time. A person was not "healed" from leprosy, but "cleansed" as from sin or other filth.

6. The leper did not doubt Jesus' power to heal, but he did doubt Jesus' willingness (5:12). What did His willingness to actually touch the leper show about . . .

Jesus' character? _____

_____

_____

_____

God's Kingdom? _____

_____

_____

_____

_____

Priest (5:14). Only the priests, acting as health inspectors, could certify a person clean of leprosy. The person then offered sacrifice in thanksgiving and was readmitted to human society and Jewish worship (Leviticus 13-14).

70

7. Jesus told the man to follow the legal requirements for certifying that Jesus had cured him.
What testimony (5:14) would this bear to the
priests and the nation?

_____

_____

_____

_____

_____

A paralytic healed (5:17-26)

Observe how differently the religious authorities
responded to Jesus.

Pharisees (5:17). There were only about six thousand Pharisees in Palestine—about one percent
of the population.[2] However, they were an
influential party because people respected them
as the "unofficial religious leaders"[3] of Judaism.
They believed that obedience to God's commands was the most important religious attitude, so in order to avoid unintentionally break-
ing a command they "fenced" the Law with
interpretations. For instance, to avoid using
God's name in vain, they never used it. These
interpretations of the Law had been handed
down as traditions for generations, so they were
regarded as just as authoritative as the Scripture
itself.[4]

Teachers of the law (5:17). These men, also called
"scribes," interpreted and taught both the written Law of Scripture and the oral law of tradition. Most of the teachers belonged to the party
of the Pharisees.[5]

Roof (5:19). "A typical Palestinian house had a flat
roof accessible by means of an outside staircase.
The roof was often made of a thick layer of clay
(packed with a stone roller), supported by mats
of branches across wood beams."[6]

71

For Thought and Discussion: Was the faith Jesus commended (5:20) necessary for forgiveness of sins? Why or why not?

Optional Application: Whom could you carry in faith to Jesus, as the paralytic's friends did? How could you do this?

8. According to 5:20, why did Jesus declare the paralytic's sins forgiven?

_____

_____

_____

Blasphemy (5:21). Pharisees considered this the worst sin a person could commit. It included any offense to God's authority or majesty. According to Jewish theology, not even the Messiah could forgive sins, so Jesus was claiming the authority of God alone.[7]

9. Jesus had a second reason for forgiving and healing the paralytic. What did these deeds prove, and how did they prove it (5:21-26)?

_____

_____

_____

_____

_____

_____

Jesus and sinners (5:27-32)

Levi collected customs duties at a toll booth outside town. He was employed by someone who had bid for the job from Rome. Levi's apostolic name was Matthew (Matthew 9:9), just as Simon's apostolic name was Peter.[8]

10. Levi's decision to abandon his toll booth meant the permanent loss of his job, for his employer would not have received him back. What does Levi's choice show about discipleship (5:27-28)?

_____

72

_____

_____

_____

_____

For Further Study:
Compare Levi's
actions to Elisha's in
1 Kings 19:19-21.

**For Thought and
Discussion:** Levi
invited all his old
friends to a party to
meet Jesus (5:29).
Does Levi offer any
example for modern
Christians? If so, what
is it?

Sinners (5:30). The Pharisees applied this label to
tax collectors, robbers, adulterers, prostitutes,
shepherds, and anyone else who did not follow
the Law of Moses according to the the interpretations of the elders.[9]

11. What must the Pharisees have believed (about
God, sin, righteousness) that made them consider it wrong to eat with sinners (5:30)?

_____

_____

_____

_____

_____

12. What does Jesus' reply to the Pharisees reveal
about His mission (5:31-32)?

_____

_____

_____

_____

_____

13. Jesus has spoken of Himself as a physician
twice (4:23, 5:31). Recall that "salvation" refers
to all kinds of healing and deliverance. What
sorts of healing has Luke recorded so far
(4:33-35,38-41; 5:8,13,20,24,27-28)?

_____

73

Optional
Application: a. Have
you experienced
Jesus' healing work?
If so, how can you
respond now?

b. How can you
follow Levi's (5:29) or
Jesus' (5:29,31)
example with regard
to sinners around
you? How can you
avoid acting toward
sinners as the Phari-
sees did?

14. Think about what Jesus does in 5:1-32 and how
each person responds. How would you summarize what this passage contributes to the message of the gospel? See 5:10,20,24,29,31-32.

_____

_____

_____

_____

_____

15. a. If you are not working on question 5 this
week, choose one truth from 5:12-32 that you
would like to apply. Write it down, along
with a verse reference.

_____

_____

_____

_____

b. What implications does this truth have for
your thoughts and actions? (Remember
SPECK from page 60.)

_____

_____

_____

_____

c. Specifically how can you act on those implications this week? (Ask God for guidance and
ability.)

_____

_____

_____

_____

_____

Study Skill—Application

It is often easiest to plan an application in
several steps, as question 15 does. Consider
these steps:

1. What truth from the passage do I want
   to apply?
2. How it this truth relevant to me? How do
   I fall short in this area, or how do I want
   to grow?
3. What can I do, by God's grace, to grow
   in this area or apply this truth?

Remember to rely on God's guidance and
power to choose and fulfill your application.
Expect to fail, confess, and repent frequently
as you grow.

16. List any questions you have about 5:1-32.

_____

_____

_____

_____

For the group

Warm-up. Ask the group to take a minute to recall
the last time Jesus confronted each of you as Lord
or as Savior.

Read aloud and summarize.

The first disciples. When you discuss a scene in a Gospel, it often helps to begin with the observations that the study guide doesn't ask specific questions about. You can ask a series of observation questions (Where does the scene take place? Who is there? What is Jesus doing at the beginning? What does He do next? How does Simon respond? etc.). Or, you can ask someone to tell the story in his or her own words. If you have someone tell the story, the rest of the group can add observations that are omitted. This will give the group a much more vivid and detailed impression of the event.

Question 3b is not mere speculation; the whole point of the event was to make Simon Peter recognize that he was a sinner and Jesus was Lord, and the point of including it in the Gospel was to help us recognize the same truth. Therefore, we need to consider why a miracle of fish worked for Simon. You can compare what happened to you that convicted you of your sinfulness and Jesus' Lordship.

Question 4 tries to bring out the fact that a conviction of the need to repent (turn around) and follow Jesus as Lord is the first step of discipleship. In other words, Jesus cannot be Simon's Savior until Simon acknowledges Jesus as Lord. In this story Jesus acts as Savior when He says, "Don't be afraid"; with those words He receives the repentant sinner into relationship with Himself. You can look for times when Jesus acts as Savior and as Lord in each of the scenes in Luke, and you can observe the ways each person responds to His claim to be Savior and Lord.

Don't forget to apply the story to yourselves in specific, reasonable ways. For instance, it may not be reasonable to conclude, "I need to go out and win some souls this week." It may be more reasonable to decide, "I am going to pray every day that Jesus will show me how to follow Him today, and especially that He will show me opportunities to lead other people to know Him as Savior and Lord. This will be more than just a quick, one-time prayer; I am going to meditate on 5:10-11 for five or ten minutes each day."

Leper, paralytic, sinners. Again, in each case 1) make observations or retell the story, 2) discuss

76

the interpretation questions in the study guide, and 3) make applications. Put yourselves in the place of the person being healed (the leper, the paralytic, Levi, Levi's friends), then in the place of the other people in the scene (the bystanders, the paralytic's friends, the Pharisees), and finally in Jesus' place. As Christians, we move from receiving salvation like the people who were healed to bringing others to salvation like the paralytic's friends and Levi. Often this latter stage involves our being in Jesus' place, touching lepers and eating with sinners. Look for specific, concrete ways you can apply these lessons either individually or as a group.

Summarize.

Wrap-up.

Worship. Praise Jesus for His authority over nature, work, health, and sin. Thank Him for forgiving your sin and inviting you to be His disciples. Ask the Savior and Lord to show you the lepers, paralytics, and sinners in your church, workplace, or community. Ask Him to enable you to love them as He does and to "catch" them for His Kingdom.

1. Marshall, page 202.
2. F. F. Bruce, *New Testament History* (Garden City, New York: Doubleday and Company, 1980), page 39 gives estimates for the population of Palestine ranging from 500,000 to 1,500,000. We don't know how many of these were Jews and how many were Gentiles. *The NIV Study Bible*, page 1547 says there were 6,000 Pharisees.
3. Morris, page 116.
4. *The NIV Study Bible*, page 1547.
5. *The NIV Study Bible*, page 1547.
6. *The NIV Study Bible*, page 1495.
7. *The NIV Study Bible*, pages 1495, 1527, 1547-1548.
8. *The NIV Study Bible*, page 1496.
9. *The NIV Study Bible*, page 1496.

LUKE 5:33-6:16

New Wine

So far, Jesus has shocked the religious establishment by acknowledging Gentiles, forgiving sin, and eating with sinners. He has refused to teach and heal according to men's ideas of God's rules. Far from avoiding confrontation, Jesus now continues to let His demonstration of the Kingdom collide with traditional views.

Read 5:33-6:16, looking for what's new in the Kingdom.

Fasting (5:33-39)

One reason why Jesus and His disciples feasted was because they wanted to be where sinners were (5:29-32). But there was a deeper reason.

Disciples (5:33). A learner, the follower of a rabbi (master, teacher). A disciple in rabbinic Judaism was bound closely to his master. The master was the disciple's sole authority for truth and model for life. However, Jesus took the relationship beyond Jewish tradition. For example, Jesus required that His disciples' allegiance to Him surpass their allegiance to family, the Law, and even life itself (6:5, 14:26-27).[1]

Fast and pray (5:33). All Jews fasted yearly on the Day of Atonement (Leviticus 16:29). Individuals

79

chose to fast at other times for worship or prayer; both the Pharisees and John's disciples did so frequently. Jesus fasted in the desert (4:2) and after the Last Supper (22:16,18). Matthew 6:16-18 assumes that Jesus' disciples will fast.

Bridegroom (5:34). In the Old Testament, God describes Himself alone, not even the Messiah, as Israel's Bridegroom (Isaiah 54:5-8, Ezekiel 16:1-63, Hosea 2:18-21).[2]

1. Why was fasting inappropriate while Jesus was present? (That is, what was Jesus saying in 5:34 about Himself and the Kingdom?)

_____

_____

_____

_____

_____

Wineskins (5:37). Wine was kept in goatskin bags. "As the fresh grape juice fermented, the wine would expand, and the new wineskin would stretch. But a used skin, already stretched, would break."[3]

2. Jesus addressed 5:36-38 to people who found His lifestyle not properly religious (5:33). Read 5:36-38 several times and reflect on what it is saying.

a. Old garments tear when patched, and old wineskins break when refilled. Therefore, what should a person do when offered a new coat or new wine?

_____

_____

80

_____

_____

b. How is this like what we should do when
offered the Kingdom?

_____

_____

_____

_____

c. Why do people sometimes prefer to patch
their old coats, keep their old wineskins
along with the new wine, or simply insist
that the "old wine is better" without even
tasting the new?

_____

_____

_____

_____

_____

_____

3. Do Jesus' words in 5:34-39 convict you in any
area of your life? If so, how are you convicted,
and what can you do about this?

_____

_____

_____

_____

_____

_____

_____

Optional Application: Ask God to show you if you are clinging to any comfortable old practice or belief that contradicts the ways of the Kingdom. Ask Him to lead you to repentance in any area He reveals to you.

The Sabbath (6:1-11)

New wineskins, new clothes, feasting—these are appropriate responses to Jesus' presence. Next, Jesus reveals what the Sabbath means in God's Kingdom.

Sabbath (6:1). The Sabbath has a rich meaning in Scripture. It commemorates God's rest from the work of Creation (Genesis 2:2-3, Exodus 20:11) and His act of freeing Israel from slavery (Deuteronomy 5:15). Each Sabbath, the people received a foretaste of the heavenly rest and liberty forfeited in the Fall (Genesis 3:16-19) but promised in God's Kingdom (Isaiah 32:1-4, 14-20). The book of Hebrews declares that Christians can live daily in God's salvation-rest while they await its final fulfillment (Hebrews 4:1-11).

Unlawful (Luke 6:2). To the Pharisees, however, the command to rest on the Sabbath had become less a foretaste of the Kingdom than a rule to prove one's obedience to God. To assure that no one violated the Fourth Commandment not to work on the Sabbath, the rabbis had specified every possible action permitted or forbidden on that day. Picking, rubbing, and eating even a few grains was equivalent to reaping, threshing, and preparing food—all manifestly work. The disciples' action would have been lawful on any other day; it was called "gleaning" the fields (Deuteronomy 23:25).

What David did (Luke 6:3). When David and his men were hungry, they accepted holy bread from the tabernacle (1 Samuel 21:1-9) even though it was unlawful for anyone but the priests to eat it (Leviticus 24:5-9). David judged that true human need outweighed the ritual law.

---

4. According to the Pharisees, a person should be allowed to go hungry rather than to glean on the Sabbath (Luke 6:1-2). How did this view of God's Sabbath miss its true significance?

_____

_____

_____

_____

_____

_____

83

For Further Study:
Compare Luke 6:1-11 to Isaiah 58:6-7, 13.

For Further Study:
Make a list of all the things the Pharisees wanted Jesus to do or not do that Jesus rejected. Then list why each thing is or isn't appropriate for the Kingdom.

5. Jesus defended not only His motives but also His authority to let His disciples glean on the Sabbath (6:5). What did He claim, and why was His claim significant?

_____

_____

_____

_____

Looking for a reason to accuse (6:7). The first time Jesus healed on the Sabbath (4:31-37), people were so awed by His power that they failed to notice He had worked on the Sabbath. The Pharisees soon noticed, however, and they eventually set up a test for Jesus' attitude toward the Sabbath laws. The Pharisees' interpretation permitted medical aid only when a life might be lost if a doctor's work were postponed until sunset. The shriveled hand was not life-threatening, so it should not be healed on the Sabbath.

6. What was Jesus saying in 6:9 about the Sabbath's purpose? Why was healing appropriate on the Sabbath?

_____

_____

_____

_____

_____

_____

7. Jesus rejected the idea that it would honor God to leave people hungry or maimed on His holy day. Are there any lessons here for your view of God, your priorities, or your use of God's day? If so, what lessons do you see?

_____

_____

_____

_____

_____

_____

_____

_____

_____

Optional Application: Write down a specific way you could apply one of the lessons you wrote in question 7. For example, how can you celebrate God's Sabbath of rest and liberation, a foretaste of the Kingdom?

For Further Study: How did Jesus prepare to choose His special ambassadors (verse 12)? What can you learn from this preparation?

The Twelve (6:12-16)

Twelve (6:13). For Jews, the number twelve symbolized the nation of Israel, the chosen people. Every Israelite belonged to one of the twelve tribes of Israel, each of which descended from one of the twelve sons of Jacob-Israel (Genesis 49:1-28). Jesus intended His twelve apostles to be the founding fathers of the Church, the new Israel, as the twelve patriarchs had been for the old Israel.[5]

Apostle (6:13). "One who is sent," a herald, ambassador, or proxy. The Twelve were going to be Jesus' special representatives to the world as well as the leaders of His Church. To equip them to fulfill this role, Jesus spent most of the rest of His ministry carefully training and disclosing Himself to them. After Jesus' death, others in the Church, such as Paul, were recognized as apostles. For the background of the word *apostle*, see the box on page 90.

Zealot (6:15). There were four main parties within Judaism in Jesus' time: Pharisees, Sadducees, Essenes, and Zealots. The Zealots were devout Jews, as devoted to the Law as the Pharisees were. In fact, Zealots were so passionate about God's lordship over the Jews that they considered it unlawful to acknowledge the

For Further Study: If you are keeping an outline as described on pages 53-54, add to it a summary of 5:1-6:16.

sovereignty of Gentile rulers, since God alone was Israel's King. Therefore, they opposed paying taxes to Rome (20:22) and often rioted when a census was taken for tax purposes. Whereas the Pharisees were content to stay out of politics and wait for God to expel the Romans, the Zealots felt called to actively help God liberate Israel.[6]

The Jewish historian Josephus called the Zealots "bandits" (Mark 15:7, John 18:40), a term that meant "insurgents" when used to describe the patriotic Zealot resistance.[7] According to Josephus, in the 50s AD Zealots systematically assassinated many Jewish leaders who cooperated with Rome, for they were as opposed to oppression from rich Jews as they were to Roman occupation.[8]

We can only imagine how Simon the Zealot may have gotten along with a bunch of apolitical Galilean fishermen and even a former tax collector, Levi. Jesus' attitudes toward the Law, Gentiles, violence, politics, and many other matters must have shaken Simon's Zealot beliefs.

Iscariot (6:16). This probably means "the man from Kerioth,"[9] a town in Judea. Judas may have been the only Judean among the apostles. His decision in 22:1-6 suggests that his political feelings leaned toward the Judean leaders and against Simon's Zealot friends.

Review

Occasionally, it is a good idea to crystallize what you've learned.

8. What is the main message you see in 5:33-6:16?

_____

_____

_____

_____

_____

9. Now try to summarize what 5:1-6:16 has revealed about . . .

Jesus' character

_____

_____

_____

_____

_____

_____

_____

Jesus' mission and the message of the Kingdom

_____

_____

_____

_____

_____

_____

_____

_____

Jesus' identity and authority

_____

_____

_____

_____

_____

_____

proper responses to Jesus

_____

_____

_____

_____

_____

_____

_____

10. Is there any way you'd like to apply some
    insight you've had while summarizing these
    passages? If so, write down your plan for prayer,
    action, or change of heart.

_____

_____

_____

_____

_____

_____

_____

11. List any questions you have about 5:33-6:16.

_____

_____

_____

_____

For the group

Warm-up. What is one new way of acting or thinking that Jesus' presence has brought to your life?

Read aloud.

Summarize.

Fasting, the Sabbath, the Twelve. The common thread in these scenes is newness—life in the Kingdom is going to have an unprecedented attitude of rejoicing, a restored celebration of the Sabbath-rest, a different leadership and membership. In each scene, bring out the contrast between the Pharisees' old ways and Jesus' new ways. Notice that Jesus doesn't reject fasting and the Sabbath, but He does reject the Pharisees' interpretations. He doesn't dismiss the twelve patriarchs who headed Israel, but He adds to them the twelve apostles who head the New Israel. Try to put yourselves in the Pharisees' place, looking for the part of you that wants to make idols of familiar interpretations and ways. Consider this framework for discussing each scene:

> What did the Pharisees want Jesus to do?
> What did Jesus do?
> Why did Jesus do this? What was He showing about the Kingdom by doing this?
> How can we act in light of this truth about the Kingdom?

Summarize. After you summarize 5:33-6:16, question 9 gives you a chance to pull together everything you've studied so far. Don't worry if you can't state the definitive word on each topic and include every detail in your summaries. Look for the big picture.

Wrap-up. This may be a good time to evaluate how well your group has been functioning during the last six meetings. You could look at the goals you set in lesson one and discuss how well you are meeting them and how you could meet them better. Or, you could discuss these questions: "What did you like best about this meeting? What did you like least? How can we do better?"

Worship. Thank God for the newness of His Kingdom. Ask Him to enable you to let go of whatever you need to lay aside. Thank Him for the message of salvation, the good news of the Kingdom, and the coming of Jesus.

The Shaliach

The word *apostolos* occurs just once in the Septuagint (the Greek Old Testament); in 1 Kings 14:6 it names a person sent with a message. However, the Septuagint does use the verb *apostello*, "to send" (Hebrew: *shalach*) seven hundred times in the sense of authorizing a messenger (Joshua 1:16, 2 Kings 19:4). *Apostolos* seems to have been the term Greek-speaking Jews used for the Jewish legal institution of the *shaliach*.

In Jewish law, the *shaliach* was "a person acting with full authority for another"[10]—an ambassador or proxy. A *shaliach* could stand in for either party in a betrothal, or deliver a certificate of divorce. A rabbi sent by the Sanhedrin (the high council in Jerusalem) to inspect synagogues or collect tithes was a *shaliach*. The leader of synagogue prayer was a *shaliach* for the group. Thus, when Luke 6:13 says Jesus named the Twelve "apostles," we can suspect that in their own language He named them His *shaluchim*.

1. Dietrich Muller, "Disciple," *The New International Dictionary of New Testament Theology*, volume 1, pages 480-490.
2. Marshall, page 225.
3. *The NIV Study Bible*, page 1455.
4. *The NIV Study Bible*, page 1460.
5. Wilcock, pages 75-78.
6. Bruce, page 96.
7. Bruce, page 98.
8. Bruce, pages 99-100.
9. Bruce, page 184.
10. Erich von Eicken and Helgo Lindner, "Apostle," *The New International Dictionary of New Testament Theology*, volume 1, page 128; see also Marshall, page 238.

LUKE 6:17-49

Kingdom People

The Pharisees had strong opinions about how
members of God's chosen people should behave. A
good Israelite should never claim God's prerogatives
(5:21), avoid sinners (5:30), fast and pray diligently
(5:33), and do nothing on the Sabbath even if another person had to suffer (6:1-11). In contrast to
these laws, Jesus declared different standards for
God's Kingdom. The standards of the Kingdom led
Jesus to heal, forgive, embrace, reconcile, and celebrate with all comers. The newness of the Kingdom
also required Jesus to choose twelve new leaders for
it. Now, in 6:17-49 we find Jesus spelling out the
laws of the Kingdom more fully.

Like Moses (Exodus 34:29-32), Jesus ascends a
mountain to be with God and descends to declare
His Law (Luke 6:12,17).[1] But the "new commandment" (John 13:34), "the royal law" (James 2:8), is
not like the old. Read 6:17-49.

Kingdom values (6:17-26)

Crowds of both Jews and Gentiles have come from
as far away as Sidon to see Jesus (6:17). Notice why
they have come (6:18-19).

Blessed (6:20). "Happy," "joyful," not because of
luck or fortune, but because of divine favor, par-
ticularly salvation.[2]

91

For Further Study:
a. Luke 16:1-31 shows how rich people can avoid the danger of riches. (See also 12:13-34, 18:18-30, 19:1-9.)
b. Luke 12:22-34 reveals wrong attitudes to which the poor are susceptible.

For Thought and Discussion: Jesus did not deny that wealth and respectability were blessings, but what did He regard as the greater blessing (6:20,23)?

Woe (6:24). "Alas"; this word expresses "pity for those who stand under judgment,"[3] compassion, not an angry threat.

1. Jesus begins His sermon by contrasting two kinds of people (6:20-26). He discusses each in four parallel ways. Describe each type of person (Blessed are you who . . .), and explain what Jesus promised them (for you . . .).

Blessed are	for you

But woe to	for you

Rich (6:24). Jesus' contemporaries assumed that wealth, health, happiness, and good reputation were signs of God's favor. Since God had promised these blessings to those who kept His covenant (Deuteronomy 28:1-14), people reasoned that anyone who had these earthly blessings must have God's favor. Even though the book of Job made clear that God had reasons for allowing favored people to suffer, and the prophets warned prosperous people about God's disfavor, still most Jews failed to hear this message.

2. Why is the Kingdom given to disciples who are poor and rejected for Jesus' sake, while people who are rich and respected are in grave danger?

_____

_____

_____

_____

_____

_____

3. a. Think about the extent to which you are poor, troubled, and rejected for Jesus' sake. How does 6:20-23 affect your attitude toward your condition? How are you inclined to act in response?

_____

_____

_____

_____

_____

_____

b. Consider the extent to which you are comfortable and respected. What attitudes does 6:24-26 move you to pray for and act on? Do any specific actions come to mind?

_____

_____

_____

_____

_____

_____

For Thought and Discussion: What attitudes (toward self, the world, God) tempt rich and respected people to lose the greatest blessing? (*Optional:* See Deuteronomy 8:17-18; 9:4; Luke 8:14; 12:21,34.)

For Thought and Discussion: How can we be sure that we are rejected "because of the Son of Man" (6:22) and not for some other reason?

For Further Study:
It has been said that
6:29-30 is irrational.
That is, a person who
obeys 6:29-30 runs a
great risk of losing
what every normal
person wants to gain.

a. What do we
risk by obeying
6:29-30?

b. What does
6:20-26 say about the
value of what we are
risking?

c. Summarize the
attitudes toward pos-
sessions and people
that Jesus commends
in 6:29b-30.

d. Luke
12:4-7,27-31 further
shows why we can
take the risk of Luke
6:27-36.

e. How does
Jesus respond to
blows in John
18:22-24, 19:1-4;
Luke 23:34?

The law of love (6:27-42)

Having turned the world's values upside down,
Jesus proceeds to overturn the world's standard of
fairness.

But I tell you (6:27). The Law of Moses laid down
the rights and duties of justice—what each person owed another. For example, the Law
required penalties proportionate to the crime
and fair repayment of loans. Jesus does not
reject the Mosaic definition of justice; fair is
still fair in law court and marketplace. But in
private relations between individuals, Jesus lays
down a new law.

---

4. In general, what is Jesus' rule for life (6:27-36)?

_____

_____

_____

_____

_____

5. From 6:27-36, explain what you think it means
to love your enemies. (What is love? Who are
your enemies?)

_____

_____

_____

_____

_____

_____

_____

_____

Sons of the Most High (6:35). The Semitic expression "son of . . ." means something like "one who has the character of. . . ." A "son of peace" (10:6 KJV, NASB, RSV) is a person who is characterized by peace, and a "son of perdition" (John 17:12 KJV) is a man whose character has destined him for destruction. Thus, in Luke 6:35, "sons of the Most High" are people who have God's character of mercy. However, in this case the sonship is more than just a figure of speech; it is a real adoption as heirs (Romans 8:14-17).

6. Jesus gives several reasons why we should treat others with love rather than strict justice. List as many as you can find in 6:32-36.

_____

_____

_____

_____

_____

_____

_____

_____

Study Skill—Context
It is crucial to read individual commands in light of the whole passage, the entire book, and the rest of Scripture. The command, "Do not judge" (Luke 6:37) is a good example. Elsewhere, Jesus commands us to discern right from wrong in ourselves and others (Matthew 7:15-20; Luke 6:43-45, 7:43, 12:57; compare Acts 4:19). Therefore, we must understand the word "judge" in light of Luke 6:27-36. Here, to judge is to pass

(continued on page 96)

Optional Application: What "measure" (6:38) do you use in evaluating and treating family members, friends, co-workers, etc.? In return, are you getting what Jesus says you deserve? In what ways do you need to change the standard by which you measure out love, judgment, giving, and forgiveness to others? Talk to God about this.

(continued from page 95)

judgment on someone, to declare what he justly deserves, and furthermore to wish heartily that he will get what is coming to him. Jesus warns against judging that someone is your enemy, that he deserves to be hated, cursing, mistreating, striking, or robbing you (6:27-29). Context also shows us that judgment and condemnation are the opposites of love, mercy, giving, and forgiving.

Luke 6:39-45 provides more context by which to interpret Jesus' command not to judge.

7. In 6:37-38, Jesus reveals a spiritual principle as a further reason why we should treat others as we would like to be treated, not as they deserve to be treated. What is that principle?

_____

_____

_____

_____

_____

8. With three illustrations, Jesus finishes putting His disciples in the proper frame of mind regarding fellow disciples' faults.

a. What will happen if you try to be your brother's spiritual guide and judge while you are blind to your own weaknesses (6:39)?

_____

_____

_____

b. What is each disciple's goal (6:40; compare 6:35-36)?

_____

_____

c. What folly does Jesus ridicule in 6:41-42?

_____

_____

_____

d. How does this warning in 6:41-42 apply to you?

_____

_____

_____

Integrity (6:43-49)

9. With the warnings of 6:37-42 in mind, we are equipped to evaluate ourselves and others when necessary. How can we recognize the state of our hearts (6:43-45)?

_____

_____

_____

_____

10. Jesus rebuked the Pharisees for self-righteous, hypocritical, judgmental, and unloving obedience to their own interpretations of God's Law. However, observe what Jesus says about obedience to *His* Law (6:46-49). How is obeying Jesus like building your house on a rock?

_____

_____

_____

_____

Optional Application: Which of the reasons in 6:32-42 most motivates you to live by 6:27-42? Ask the Lord to impress this truth on your heart. You might plan to meditate on the relevant verse for a few days.

Optional Application: Evaluate your own heart by the standard of 6:45.
   a. What areas of your heart need forgiveness and cleansing? Ask God to do this.
   b. How does this evaluation affect your desire to judge or forgive others' words and actions?

For Thought and Discussion: Moses told Israel to obey God, not Moses, as Lord. What does Jesus claim in 6:46?

97

11. a. Examine the fruits of your life prayerfully as you reread 6:17-49. What one insight from 6:17-49 do you most want to take to heart and act upon this week?

_____

_____

_____

_____

b. How do you fall short in this area?

_____

_____

_____

c. What specific steps, including prayer and meditation, can you take to begin putting Jesus' words into practice?

_____

_____

_____

_____

12. Summarize what 6:17-49 tells you about what a disciple of Jesus is and does.

_____

_____

_____

_____

_____

13. List any questions you have about the material in this lesson.

For Further Study: Add 6:17-49 to your outline of the book.

_____

_____

_____

_____

For the group

Warm-up. Ask everyone to think of someone he or she has something against. Don't have anyone name names, but ask everyone to keep that person in mind as you discuss 6:17-49.

Read aloud.

Summarize.

Kingdom values. Many people have preconceptions about Luke 6:20-26 that keep them from hearing what Jesus is saying to them. Some people who believe in social activism use this passage to prove that God is on the side of the poor against the rich, but they ignore that Jesus is addressing not all poor people but His committed disciples. *Their* poverty and persecution is cause for joy. On the other hand, some people who are comfortable and respectable try to gloss over Jesus' plain statement that the rich, well-fed, and respected are in grave trouble. Matthew 5:3 says "Blessed are the poor in spirit," but Luke 6:20 says flatly "Blessed are you who are poor." In short, poor people who judge rich people are not the poor Jesus loves (6:37), and middle-class people who reassure themselves that 6:24-27 is not about them are taking a risk (6:38). Encourage your group to examine and lay aside their preconceptions. Then take a hard look at what the implications of 6:20-26 might be for you.

The law of love. Again, it is tremendously tempting to soften the commands in 6:27-42. It is true that thieves and spendthrifts should not be allowed to plunder Christians; however, our motive in preventing this is not in order to guard selfishly our

99

rightful possessions, but rather to serve the good of the thief. Jesus showed this astounding attitude in His trial. Without malice, He rebuked one soldier who struck Him in order to penetrate the man's misguided anger (John 18:22-23), but He silently tolerated other abuse (John 19:1-4) and was still able to pray and die for His persecutors (Luke 23:34).

This approach to life is impossible for us without the Holy Spirit, so it can seem inconceivable. We don't stop hating, judging, or fearing by an act of will. Therefore, the questions in this lesson explore the reasons why 6:27-42 is not only realistic but essential for God's kingdom people. The goal is to change the way you think. Then try to be honest with each other about how you fall short of this standard. Take time for self-examination and confession. Plan time to pray for each other's ability to love and forgive specific people.

Integrity. Consider questions 9 and 10 in the context of poverty and love. Do your speech and behavior reveal the heart of a rich or a poor person, whatever the size of your bank account (6:45)? Do unforgiving actions contradict forgiving words, or vice versa? Are you really willing to risk building your house on the rock of Jesus' standard of love and poverty? If questions like these make your group feel guilty, point out that this is why we need a Savior, an empowering Spirit, and a Father who is "kind to the ungrateful and wicked" (6:35).

Summarize.

Wrap-up. To encourage the group as they go out to apply what they've studied, remind them that 6:20-49 is the Law of the Kingdom and emphasizes Jesus as Lord. It is an essential part of Jesus' message, but it is only a part. In lesson eight you will again focus on the good news of the Kingdom and Jesus as Savior. After grappling with His high standards, you may be glad to bask in His mercies. Then, a later lesson will look at the Holy Spirit's role in making the standards attainable.

Worship.

1. Wilcock, pages 78-79.
2. Marshall, page 248.
3. Marshall, page 255.

LUKE 7:1-23, 36-50

Good News

Jesus has already identified the people to whom the gospel is addressed—"He has anointed me to preach good news *to the poor*" (4:18). What is that news about? "I must preach the good news of *the kingdom of God*" (4:43); "Blessed are *you who are poor, for yours is the kingdom of God*" (6:20). In chapters 7 and 8 we find Jesus proceeding to make this message plainer.

Read 7:1-50, keeping in mind the teaching of chapter 6. Notice how Jesus practiced what He preached.

A centurion and his servant (7:1-10)

Centurion (7:2). Roughly equivalent to an army captain.[1] He commanded a company of a hundred troops, probably for Herod the tetrarch.[2]

1. Scripture records only two occasions on which Jesus was "amazed" (Mark 6:6, Luke 7:9). How did the centurion show the great faith that so amazed Jesus?

_____

_____

_____

Optional Application: How can you apply the centurion's example in your own life?

For Further Study: Compare Luke 7:11-17 to 1 Kings 17:9, 17-24. How did Jesus' act resemble Elijah's? Why do you think people responded as they did to Jesus' act (Luke 7:16)?

2. What example does the centurion's behavior offer us?

_____

_____

_____

_____

_____

_____

A woman and her son (7:11-17)

Widow (7:12). A woman without any males to protect her was the most helpless of people, since wage work for women was rare; yet she had more than economic reasons for grief.

Coffin (7:14). Probably an open bier holding the wrapped body, according to Jewish custom.[3] That was why the young man was able to sit up.

3. No one asked Jesus to raise the young man. According to 7:13, why did Jesus do so?

_____

_____

_____

4. Jesus' good news is for "the poor." Who are the poor who receive Jesus' ministry in . . .

7:1-10 (*Optional:* See Luke 2:30-32, Acts 10:34-35)

_____

_____

7:11-17 _____

_____

5. What is the "good news of the kingdom" that Jesus brings to these people? (Recall the meaning of salvation, page 35.)

_____

_____

_____

_____

_____

6. Think about who the poor are and what the good news is. What implications do these facts have for your life?

_____

_____

_____

_____

_____

_____

_____

For Thought and Discussion: How is Luke 7:22-23 an encouragement for believers awaiting the fulfillment of the Kingdom?

Jesus answers John (7:18-23)

Are you the one (7:19). John's doubt is understandable. He was imprisoned shortly after he baptized Jesus (3:19-20), so he could know of Jesus only what he heard. Isaiah had prophesied that the Messiah would "proclaim freedom for the prisoners" (Isaiah 61:1, Luke 4:18), but John was still in prison. Isaiah had said the Messiah would "proclaim . . . the day of vengeance of our God" (Isaiah 61:2), but John had seen no vengeance on wicked men like Herod.

7. In light of John the Baptist's preaching (Luke 3:7-9,16-18), explain what you think John was asking in Luke 7:19. What did he expect the Coming One to do?

_____

_____

_____

_____

_____

8. John knew Isaiah's prophecies in Isaiah 26:19, 29:18-19, 35:5-6, 61:1. How did Jesus confirm John's faith in Him (Luke 7:21-22)?

_____

_____

_____

_____

_____

9. Compare Isaiah 61:2 to Luke 4:19. What part of Isaiah 61:2 was Jesus fulfilling, and what part was He leaving for His future return?

fulfilling in current ministry _____

_____

_____

_____

_____

leaving for future return _____

_____

_____

_____

_____

A sinful woman (7:36-50)

We will skip over 7:24-35 for the moment in order to continue the theme of this lesson.

A woman who had lived a sinful life (7:37). A prostitute. She could easily have entered Simon's house, since dinners were not private, but she would not have been welcome.

At his feet (7:38). "People did not sit at table, but reclined on low couches, leaning on the left arm with the head towards the table and the body stretched away from it. The sandals were removed before reclining."[4] Therefore, the woman could not reach Jesus' head, the part of the body that a host normally anointed when a guest entered his house, but she could reach His feet.

The feet were considered the meanest part of the body. The lowest servant of the household had the job of washing street dirt from guests' feet when they arrived.

Hair (7:38). Considered the most glorious part of the body. A woman almost never unbound her hair in public.[5]

---

10. a. In the parable (7:41-42), what caused the man who was forgiven the five hundred denarii to love more than his fellow debtor?

_____

_____

_____

  b. At the dinner (7:36-38,44-48), what caused the prostitute to show great love?

_____

_____

_____

_____

Optional Application: With which debtor do you identify in 7:41-42? How should this parable affect your attitude toward God? How can you act on that attitude this week?

105

For Thought and Discussion: How does Jesus' behavior in 7:36-50 fit with His normally humble character?

Optional Application: What has Jesus forgiven you? In what specific ways can you respond as the prostitute did?

c. Simon showed he "loved little" by doubting Jesus' insight and purity (7:39) and by neglecting common acts of hospitality (7:44-46). According to the parable in 7:41-42, why did Simon love little?

_____

_____

_____

_____

11. Picture Jesus reclining at Simon's table, with a prostitute sobbing and kissing His feet. Jesus says, "her many sins have been forgiven—for she loved [her creditor] much" (7:47). What is Jesus claiming about Himself?

_____

_____

_____

_____

12. On what basis is the woman "forgiven" and "saved"? (On the basis of her faith, her love, God's love, Jesus' character, another reason, several reasons? Look at Luke 7:47,50; compare Romans 3:21-26, 5:6-8.)

_____

_____

_____

_____

13. a. Who is "the poor" in 7:36-50, and how does that person display poverty?

_____

_____

_____

_____

106

b. Who is "the rich" in this incident, and how does that person show it?

_____

_____

_____

_____

_____

c. What "good news of the kingdom" does the poor person receive from Jesus?

_____

_____

_____

_____

For Thought and Discussion: What does "salvation" mean for the centurion? The widow? The prostitute?

Optional Application: With whom can you share the most significant thing you learned from this lesson?

Your response

14. Review 7:1-23,36-50. Summarize what these passages show about . . .

the mission of "the one who was to come"

_____

_____

_____

_____

_____

_____

the response we should make to Him

_____

_____

_____

_____

For Thought and Discussion: Describe the character traits Jesus shows in 7:1-23,36-50.

Optional Application: Meditate on Jesus' character as 7:1-23,36-50 reveals it. Thank Him for being like this and doing what He does.

Optional Application: He who has been forgiven much loves much (7:47). Does this truth encourage you as you struggle to become the disciple Jesus described in 6:20-49? If so, how does it encourage you?

15. Is there any response that you would like to make this week to the story of the centurion, widow, or prostitute? (Perhaps you see a character trait of Jesus—a way of treating people—you want to develop. You may want to respond to Jesus with the attitude of one of the people in this chapter. You could meditate on Jesus Himself.) If so, explain what touches you most in this section and what you plan to do in response.

what touches you most

_____

_____

_____

_____

_____

_____

how you plan to respond to or apply it

_____

_____

_____

_____

_____

Study Skill—Parables

Luke 7:41-42 is a classic parable; it is a little story, not a simple comparison. When trying to interpret a true parable, keep these guidelines in mind:

1. A true parable is like a joke in that the story has one main point that the hearer should catch at once. Jesus sets up an ordinary situation, then gives it an unexpected twist to make His point.

(continued on page 109)

108

(continued from page 108)

2. A parable is not meant to be a riddle or puzzle with a hidden meaning. Instead, just as you are meant to get the point of a joke and respond with laughter and perhaps a change of heart, so the point of a parable should hit you at once, startle you into looking at things differently, and move you to respond.

3. In order to "get" a joke about a traveling salesman, you have to know something about the culture. Likewise, in order to get the point of a parable, you have to understand relevant parts of Jewish culture.

4. A parable is not an allegory, where every element has symbolic meaning. Rather, it has "points of reference"[6] on which the story hinges and a single "point" that calls for a response.[7] The points of reference are chosen to draw the audience into the story so that they will respond when they get the point.

For instance, in Luke 7:41-42, the points of reference are the moneylender (=God) and the two debtors (=Simon and the prostitute). The parable startles each hearer and demands a response: unloving Simon needs to repent of ingratitude toward God and scorn toward "sinners"; the loving prostitute needs to go in peace and joy, knowing that she is forgiven. For us, the question is, "Am I like Simon or the prostitute?" If the parable were an allegory, then everything, even the 50 and 500 denarii, would have symbolic meaning.

16. List any questions you have about 7:1-23,36-50.

_____

_____

_____

_____

_____

_____

For the group

Warm-up. Ask each person to tell one thing that happened when he or she tried to apply Jesus' teaching in 6:17-49. If (as is likely), some members of the group were less than successful, encourage each other and make any practical suggestions you can. However, keep this discussion brief. It should put you in the proper humble frame of mind to look at the incident with Simon the Pharisee and the prostitute.

Read aloud.

Summarize.

Questions. Having summarized the main point of the lesson, the group is in danger of taking one of two extremes. You may pay attention only to the good news to the poor in each story and so ignore the unique lessons about faith, love, etc. in each. Or, you may forget the theme you summarized and study each story in isolation. Try to avoid both these extremes.

One question that 7:47,50 often raises is, "Does Jesus save us because we show faith or forgive because we show love? Or, does He save and forgive on some other basis, hoping for a response of faith and love?" Question 12 suggests some possible answers and cross-references.

For application, ask the group to think of opportunities their current circumstances offer for showing faith in Jesus (like the centurion), love for Jesus (like the prostitute), or trust in Jesus (like John). Since faith, love, and trust are in part God's gifts, agree to pray for these traits in each other.

Summarize.

Worship.

1. Morris, pages 135-136.
2. *The NIV Study Bible*, page 1551.
3. Marshall, page 286.
4. Morris, page 147.
5. Morris, page 147.
6. Gordon D. Fee and Douglas Stuart, *How to Read the Bible for All Its Worth* (Grand Rapids, Michigan: Zondervan Corporation, 1982), page 127.
7. Fee and Stuart, page 126.

LUKE 7:24-35, 8:1-21

Responding to the News

In the last few lessons we've seen Jesus proclaim the Kingdom, perform the signs of the Kingdom, and explain the "law" of the Kingdom. Key phrases have been "preach the good news," "the poor," "the Kingdom of God," "saved," "faith," and "love." The poor have included the sick, bereaved, sinful, and even a Gentile military officer concerned for His slave.

In this lesson we'll look again (as in 6:20-49) at the response to the message of salvation that Jesus seeks. Read 7:24-35 and 8:1-21.

Jesus discusses John the Baptist
(7:24-35)

Remember that the visit from John's messengers prompted these comments from Jesus.

A reed . . . fine clothes (7:24-25). The crowds had not flocked to the wilderness to enjoy the desert plant life or to see a city gentleman. No, they had gone to hear a man whose manner was the very opposite of a quivering reed or a palace dandy.

Prophet (7:26). There may have been people with prophetic gifts for insight and prayer in Judea (Luke 2:25-32,36), but Israel had not seen a

111

prophet with a public ministry for four hundred years. As far as most people knew, biblical times were over. When John appeared, the crowds sought him because his coming was like the days of the prophets of old restored.

You (7:27). Luke 7:27 combines Exodus 23:20 and Malachi 3:1. In Exodus, the "you" is God's people; the messenger prepares their path toward the promised land. In Malachi, the messenger prepares for God's coming to His Temple.

1. The Old Testament prophets had prepared Israel to understand God's Old Testament acts. John was "more than a prophet" (Luke 7:26) because he prepared the "way" for someone (7:27).

a. Whose "way" did he prepare (Luke 3:4)?

_____

_____

_____

b. How did John prepare that person's way (3:3,7-18)?

_____

_____

_____

_____

2. John the Baptist was greatest among those "born of women" (Luke 7:28). Why is the least citizen of the Kingdom greater still (John 1:12-13, 3:5-8)?[1]

_____

_____

_____

_____

_____

112

Acknowledged that God's way was right (Luke 7:29). "Justified God" in KJV; "acknowledged God's justice" in NASB.

Optional Application: Do you ever reject God's purpose in the sense of Luke 7:30? How can you consistently acknowledge God's justice in your daily life?

3. a. How did accepting John's baptism show that the common people "acknowledged that God's way was right"?

_____

_____

_____

_____

_____

b. How did refusing baptism show that the religious leaders "rejected God's purpose for themselves" (7:30)?

_____

_____

_____

_____

_____

4. Although some people acknowledged John's and Jesus' messages, most resembled children in a bad sense.

a. Why did the people reject John when he "sang a dirge" (7:32-33), when he lived strictly and preached warning?

_____

_____

_____

_____

_____

113

b. Why did they reject Jesus when He "played the flute" (7:32,35), when He lived exuberantly and preached joy?

_____

_____

_____

_____

_____

c. What is one way in which 7:31-35 is relevant to modern people?

_____

_____

_____

_____

_____

5. What discovery in 7:24-35 seems most significant to you? If it suggests an attitude you need to change or action you need to take, write it down also.

_____

_____

_____

_____

_____

_____

On the road (8:1-3)

Jesus traveled (8:1). Luke 4:43-44 mentioned the first time Jesus traveled from town to town in the Galilean countryside. Then, for some time,

114

Jesus preached mainly in synagogues and worked from a home base in Capernaum. Now He begins a second tour of the countryside.[2]

Mary (called Magdalene) (8:2). Mary of Magdala has been equated with the prostitute of 7:36-50, but Luke makes it clear that she had been possessed by seven demons—a quite different trouble. Mary Magdalene should also not be confused with Mary of Bethany, the sister of Martha and Lazarus (John 11:1).

Helping to support them (8:3). Luke tells us more about women than Matthew, Mark, or John; we've already seen Elizabeth, Mary, Anna, Peter's mother-in-law, the widow of Nain, and a prostitute. Now, only Luke tells us how Jesus and His disciples were supported. They took no money for healing and teaching, but grateful people gave them food, money, hospitality, and service. Foremost among these supporters were some women. In Jesus' day it was somewhat startling for a rabbi to let women support Him, but it was unheard-of for a rabbi to let women travel with Him as disciples.[3]

For Thought and Discussion: What does 8:1-3 tell you about Jesus' character? About the ways of His Kingdom?

The four soils (8:4-15)

In chapter 4, Jesus proclaimed the Kingdom to the crowds. In chapter 5, He called His first disciples, but continued to work and preach publicly. The sermon of chapter 6 was delivered before the crowds (6:17) but directed especially at the disciples (6:20), for the sermon described the character of a true disciple, a citizen of God's Kingdom, a member of the New Israel built upon the foundation of the newly appointed apostles. Yet in chapter 7, Jesus worked publicly to sift out those who would respond in faith from those who would respond with criticism or indifference.

From now on, Jesus will address the crowds almost exclusively in parables. For, unlike the plain words of 4:18-21, parables both demand a response and allow an evasion; they invite the convicted to inquire further, but permit the indifferent to remain ignorant. In this way, Jesus will continue to divide disciples from religious spectators.

For Thought and Discussion: How does the sentence "He who has ears to hear, let him hear" (8:8) reinforce the point of the parable?

For Thought and Discussion: What does it mean to have "a noble and good heart" (8:15)? How can a person develop one?

Study Skill—Parables versus Allegory
Jesus said that the parable of the four soils was the key to all His parables (Mark 4:13). Therefore, He interpreted the five points of reference—the seed and the four soils.

The parable is not an allegory, for Jesus did not interpret the trampling, the moisture, and so on. Those minor details were relatively unimportant, so Jesus told the parable somewhat differently on different occasions (Mark 4:3-20, Matthew 13:3-23). Most importantly, the purpose of the parable is not so much to show us the four possible kinds of soil as to move us to *respond* to the overall message.

6. a. The audience of a parable is a clue to its interpretation, for the audience is supposed to identify with the points of reference (recall the Study Skill on pages 108-109). Who is the audience of the parable of the four soils (8:4)?

_____

b. The best way to understand the point of a parable is to read it over and over. Read 8:5-8 and 8:11-15. What main point is Jesus trying to get across to His audience?

_____

_____

_____

_____

_____

_____

To sow (8:5). "In Eastern practice the seed was sometimes sown first and the field plowed afterward. Roads and pathways went directly through many fields, and the traffic made much of the surface too hard for seed to take root in."[4]

Secrets (8:10). In the New Testament, God's secrets are truths that can be known only by revelation, truths that were previously hidden but are now revealed in the gospel.[5]

Parables (8:10). The Aramaic word for "parable" is *methal*. It means "riddle" and "puzzle" as well as "story parable." Thus, Jesus is saying that he speaks in *mathelin* (parables) because to outsiders the whole secret of the Kingdom is a *methal* (puzzle).[6]

7. a. What kind of person does God enable to understand the puzzle of the Kingdom (8:9-10; compare 5:10-11, 7:50, 8:8)?

_____

_____

_____

_____

_____

b. Most of the crowd sees and hears Jesus but does not perceive the secret of the Kingdom, the word of God. Why does God not enable such people to understand either the parables or the secret (7:31-35, 8:11-14)?

_____

_____

_____

_____

_____

8. a. What is one implication the parable of the four soils has for your life?

_____

_____

_____

Optional Application: a. This week, meditate daily on the parable of the four soils, especially 8:15, and look for ways to apply it.
b. Ask God to make you more like the good soil "with a noble and good heart" (8:15). Ask Him to help you to hear, retain, and persevere in His Word. What action can you take to learn to do this better?

Optional Application: Think about the four kinds of soil (8:11-15). Which of the first three kinds best describes what most hinders you from hearing Jesus' word, responding, and bearing a fruitful crop? What can you do about this problem?

_____

_____

b. How can you respond to the parable during the next few days or weeks?

_____

_____

_____

_____

_____

The lamp (8:16-18)

The audience of the parable in 8:16 is the disciples (and now the Church), to whom the knowledge of God's secrets has been given.

9. Jesus' earthly ministry was a mystery at the time. But did He intend His message to remain a secret forever? Why or why not (8:16-17)?

_____

_____

_____

_____

_____

10. What implications does this intention have for Jesus' disciples, who will be the only people that understand the secret once Jesus has left the world (8:16-18)?

_____

_____

_____

_____

_____

118

Listen (8:18). For the crowds, the parable of the soils was a call to a first commitment ("He who has ears to hear let him hear"). For the disciples, it was a call to listen even more carefully than they already had.

Jesus' true family (8:19-21)

Jesus did not reject His natural family, even though at this time His relatives did not believe in Him (Mark 3:21,31-32). Rather, He took an opportunity to reinforce a lesson for His disciples.

11. Whom does Jesus recognize as His true family (8:21)?

_____

_____

_____

12. How would you summarize the point of 8:1-21? (Consider 8:8,10,15,16,18,21.)

_____

_____

_____

_____

13. In questions 5 and 8, you described some ways you could apply 7:24-35 and 8:4-15. If, after considering 8:16-21, you now have a clearer idea of what you want to pray about and put into practice this week, write down what you want to do.

_____

_____

_____

_____

For Thought and Discussion: a. Why must both inquirer and disciple take care to respond to whatever knowledge of God's truth they do have (8:18)?

b. What does 8:18 imply for your life?

119

For Further Study:
Add 7:1-50 and
8:1-21 to your outline
of Luke's Gospel. How
do these chapters
contribute to the
overall message?

14. List any questions you have about 7:24-35 or
8:1-21.

_____

_____

_____

_____

For the group

Warm-up. Ask everyone to remember the last time
he or she gave someone instructions and that person didn't listen accurately. Let one or two people
share their stories briefly.

Read aloud.

Summarize.

Jesus discusses John. Ask the group why they think
Luke spends so much time on John the Baptist.
Why is 7:24-35 important to the Gospel? One reason
is that Jesus' contemporaries often compared John
and Jesus. Some thought that the two men's messages were contradictory (7:31-35), others rejected
both men (7:30), some acclaimed both for a time
but later grew disillusioned (7:29, 23:35), and a very
few perceived the connection between John's and
Jesus' messages. As the last Old Testament prophet
and herald of the gospel, John was an important
link between old and new. John's message about
sin, judgment, and repentance was meant to soften
the people's hearts to receive Jesus' offer of salvation. What are the implications for us? How can we
be sure to hear both John's and Jesus' messages?

The four soils. Jesus told this parable to the childish
(7:31-35) crowd. The multitude had received John's
word with joy at first, but they had soon wearied of
his demands. Now Jesus asks if they will do the
same with His message. Trace the theme of hearing,
responding, and persevering through 8:4-15,
8:16-18, and 8:19-21.
   Discuss specifically how each of you can hear
God's Word and put it into practice this week. Go

through the four kinds of soil together, and let each person share the kinds of things that get in the way of his hearing, retaining, and persevering. How can you help each other to resist these hindrances? Also, what kind of crop or fruit (8:15) do you think God desires from each of you? How can you help each other to produce this? Thinking of application as a group project can sometimes help to relieve unnecessary pressure from individuals. But remember that in the end, responsiveness and fruitfulness are each person's responsibility (along with God; see John 15:1-8).

The lamp.

Jesus' family.

Summarize.

Worship. Praise God for the justice and mercy of His message through John and Jesus. Ask Him to enable you to hear and respond. Confess whatever hinders you from fruitfulness.

1. Luke 13:28 makes clear that John and the other Old Testament prophets and saints were going to enter the Kingdom of God along with the people who believed in Jesus after He came.
2. *The NIV Study Bible*, page 1553.
3. Morris, page 149.
4. *The NIV Study Bible*, page 1553.
5. *The NIV Study Bible*, pages 1500, 1553.
6. Fee and Stuart, pages 124-125.

LUKE 8:22-56

Power

In His early ministry, Jesus taught the crowds openly, but in 8:1-21 we saw Him beginning to reserve the secrets of the Kingdom for those who had responded in faith and practice to the tiny seed of God's Word. Likewise, Jesus earlier performed the signs of the Kingdom as a testimony to the crowds, but now He narrows His audience so that the signs are primarily lessons for His disciples.

In 8:22-56, Luke recounts the events of a day or two. Jesus and the disciples cross the Sea of Galilee to Gerasa, then cross back to the region of Capernaum. As you read about the four works of power in 8:22-56, ask the Lord what He wants His disciples to learn from these incidents.

A storm (8:22-25)

Squall (8:23). The Sea of Galilee, a lake 13 by 7 miles, lies about 700 feet below sea level. Cold winds often sweep down nearby mountains and whip up sudden storms.

1. What do the disciples learn about Jesus in 8:22-25?

_____

_____

123

For Further Study: Does Jesus always save us from natural disasters? Why or why not? Think about how Paul and the rest experienced Jesus' saving power at sea (Acts 27:1-28:16).

2. Jesus questions His friends' lack of faith (8:25). How does their initial response to the danger of shipwreck show a lack of faith (8:24)? Consider how they should have acted.

_____

_____

_____

_____

_____

3. Consider the four soils in 8:11-15. What hindered the disciples from producing the "fruit" of faith in the shipboard incident?

_____

_____

_____

_____

_____

A demoniac (8:26-39)

Observe the pathetic plight of the possessed man in this scene (8:27-29).

Legion (8:30). A Roman legion comprised six thousand soldiers. The demons named themselves as an army of Satan.

Abyss (8:31). The pit where evil spirits and Satan will be confined when God's Kingdom is fulfilled (Revelation 9:1-6, 20:1-10).

Pigs (8:32). Pigs were unclean and forbidden food to Jews (Leviticus 11:7-8). However, Decapolis (see the map on page 10) was a largely Gentile region. The pigs carried the demons to the bottom of the lake, symbolic of the Abyss.[1]

4. What aspect of His power did Jesus display in 8:26-33?

_____

_____

_____

_____

For Thought and Discussion: Why do you think Jesus' power terrifies some people? Try to think about what happened to the Gerasenes from their point of view (8:32-37).

5. a. How did these three groups of people respond to Jesus when they saw His power in Gerasa and on the sea?

the disciples (8:25) _____

_____

_____

_____

the Gerasenes (8:34-37) _____

_____

_____

_____

the freed demoniac (8:38-39) _____

_____

_____

_____

b. All of these are understandable human responses. How should we respond when Jesus exhibits His power in our lives (Proverbs 9:10, Luke 5:8-11, 8:38-39)?

_____

_____

_____

_____

_____

125

For Further Study:
Add 8:22-56 to your
outline of Luke's
Gospel.

**Optional
Application:** What
obstacles are you cur-
rently facing as you
try to trust Jesus in
the midst of a
difficulty?

A girl and a woman (8:40-56)

Ruler of the synagogue (8:41). He was responsible
for "conducting services, selecting participants
and maintaining order," and caring for the synagogue building.[2]

Crowds (8:42). Near Eastern towns had narrow,
winding streets that were always packed during
the day. Haste in an emergency was nearly
impossible in the face of street vendors, children, beggars, shoppers, and animals. And,
besides the normal crush, Jesus was surrounded
by a flock of inquirers and spectators.

Bleeding (8:43). Like leprosy, bleeding made a person ceremonially unclean. For twelve years this
woman had been barred from worship services,
and even her friends would have avoided touching her. She was presumptuous to defile a holy
man with her touch (Leviticus 15:25).

6. Once again, Jesus revealed His power. What
kinds of affliction did He overcome this time
(8:40-56)?

_____

_____

_____

_____

7. Jairus faced many obstacles to faith when he
brought his need to Jesus, but he persevered
(see 8:15). What obstacles tempted Jairus to
abandon hope of help from Jesus?

8:41 _____

_____

_____

8:42 _____

_____

8:43-48 _____

_____

8:49 _____

_____

8:52 _____

_____

8:53 _____

_____

For Thought and Discussion: Luke 8:22-56 gives four examples of Jesus saving people from afflictions—weather, demons, social rejection and sickness, and death. Has Jesus saved you from any afflictions? If so, how was faith necessary for your deliverance?

8. What obstacles to faith did the bleeding woman have to overcome in order to lay hold of the salvation/healing available from Jesus (8:43-48)?

_____

_____

_____

_____

_____

_____

For Thought and Discussion: a. Jesus probably knew who had touched Him and why. Why do you think He made the woman confront Him publicly (8:45-48)? What did the confrontation accomplish?
   b. What did it reveal about Jesus' character and His aims?

9. Jesus deliberately led His disciples on this journey, and even allowed three of them to witness the little girl's resurrection (8:51). How would you summarize what the disciples might have learned from the events of 8:22-56?

_____

_____

_____

_____

_____

_____

_____

127

b. What attitudes toward people did Jesus model for His disciples by the way He treated the demoniac, Jairus, the bleeding woman, and Jairus' daughter?

Optional Application: Meditate on 8:39, 8:48, or 8:50. Think about how Jesus' words apply to you.

10. Consider one or two of the trials you and those around you face. How does 8:22-56 urge you to think, pray, and act in those specific situations?

_____

_____

_____

_____

_____

_____

_____

11. List any questions you have about 8:22-56.

_____

_____

_____

_____

For the group

Warm-up. Ask the group, "What is the worst trial you or others close to you are facing?"

Read aloud.

Summarize.

Questions. The main ideas in this lesson are:

1. What does each scene reveal about Jesus?
2. How can we respond rightly to trials?
3. What obstacles to faith in the midst of tribulation do people in each scene experience, and what can we learn from their responses?

Don't feel limited to these main ideas. Use the stories in this lesson to suggest ways you can deal with the specific trials you are facing. Help the group to identify with the disciples in the boat, the demoniac, Jairus, and the bleeding woman. (How might you have felt in their places? How are their responses to Jesus models for you?)

Summarize.

Wrap-up.

Worship. Thank God for providing deliverance from and strength in the midst of affliction. Praise Him for His power over all that assails you.

1. *The NIV Study Bible,* page 1454.
2. *The NIV Study Bible,* page 1503, 1555.

LUKE 9:1-17

Imitating Jesus

Jesus' ministry in Galilee is drawing to a close. He has proclaimed the Kingdom of God, the good news of salvation, to the crowds by word and deed. Those who troubled to ask Jesus to interpret His words or use His power have received from Him. Those who have not bothered to ask have received little. His ministry has been a puzzle or an offense to most of His hearers, but a few have responded and become disciples. From these He has chosen twelve to lead and represent the Church He is inaugurating. From now on, He will focus His efforts not on inviting the crowd but on training the disciples, especially their twelve leaders.

In 9:1-50, Luke pulls together the strands of his story so far. Read the whole passage, looking for these two themes: Who is Jesus? and, Who are the disciples?

The Twelve sent (9:1-6)

1. When Jesus called the Twelve, He then *gave* to them and *sent* them (9:1-2).

   a. What did Jesus give them?

   _____

   _____

   _____

Optional Application: In what general ways does the disciples' mission apply to Christians? In what specific ways does it apply to you? How can you act on your mission in the next few weeks? (Talk to God about this.)

b. What did He send them to do?

_____

_____

_____

_____

2. How was the mission of the Twelve related to Jesus' own mission? (Compare 7:22, 8:1, 9:2.)

_____

_____

_____

_____

3. What was Jesus' goal in training His disciples (6:40, 24:46-48; Matthew 28:18-20)?

_____

_____

_____

_____

_____

4. Glance over 5:1-9:6. What methods has Jesus used so far to train His disciples? (For instance, see 5:1-11; 6:20-49; 8:1,51).

_____

_____

_____

_____

_____

_____

Shake the dust off (9:5). Jews shook the dust of Gentile cities from their feet before returning to their land; Gentile dust would have defiled the ritually clean land of a holy people.[1] The Twelve were to testify that Jewish towns who rejected the good news were unrighteous before God.

Herod's question (9:7-9)

5. Jesus had been raising a stir in Herod's territory, and many rumors were plaguing the tetrarch's guilty conscience (9:7-8). What question worried him (9:9)?

_____

_____

_____

Five thousand fed (9:10-17)

Having fulfilled their mission as Jesus' heralds, the Twelve are now rightly called "apostles" (9:10). Jesus takes them across the lake alone to rest and reflect (Mark 6:31), but the crowds follow. Rest and reflection are important parts of training, especially after a strenuous practice session several weeks in length. But Jesus postpones His students' rest for one more day to teach them some important lessons. The feeding of the five thousand is the only miracle recorded in all four Gospels.

6. What attitudes toward needy people does Jesus model for His disciples?

9:11 _____

_____

_____

9:12-13 _____

_____

_____

For Thought and Discussion: a. Why were preaching the Kingdom and healing the sick both parts of the Twelve's mission (9:2)? (Consider 4:18-19, 5:17-25.)

b. Why did Jesus command the Twelve to conduct their mission as in 9:3-5?

For Thought and Discussion: How do we know when to keep laboring for the Kingdom and when to pause for rest and reflection (9:10-11)? How do we deal with the seemingly endless needs of the people around us?

7. a. The disciples had taken no provisions for food or shelter on their practice mission (9:3), but the people they met had presumably fed and housed them. What should the disciples have learned from their experience in the villages?

_____

_____

_____

_____

   b. Now Jesus offers the disciples a chance to put the lesson from their experience into practice. From 9:12-13, do they seem to have learned that lesson? How can you tell?

_____

_____

_____

_____

   c. How does the feeding of the five thousand reinforce the lesson the disciples should have learned (9:16-17)?

_____

_____

_____

_____

_____

About fifty each (9:14). Mark says "groups of hundreds and fifties" (Mark 6:40). Jesus deliberately reenacted Israel's wilderness wandering with Moses. At that time, the Israelites camped

134

in groups of hundreds and fifties (Exodus 18:21). God used Moses to feed the people miraculously with manna (Exodus 16). John's Gospel shows Jesus explicitly connecting His feeding of the five thousand with the miracle of the manna (John 6:1-15,25-59).

The prophet Elisha also miraculously fed a hundred men (2 Kings 4:42-44). Therefore, the Jews concluded that Jesus was the great Prophet like Moses whom Moses foretold (Deuteronomy 18:15, John 6:14).

For Thought and Discussion: Does question 9 suggest any implications for our partnership with Jesus in performing His works? If so, what are they?

8. What do you think Jesus wanted the feeding of the five thousand to teach the disciples about Him?

_____

_____

_____

_____

Twelve basketfuls (9:17). Jews regarded bread as God's gift, so tradition dictated that scraps which fell on the ground be picked up after a meal. Everybody carried small wicker baskets in which to collect the bits of bread.[2] Each of the Twelve returned with his basket full, ready to provide for others again.[3]

9. Previously, the disciples watched while Jesus performed the signs of the Kingdom. This time, what part did each play in the work (9:12-17)?

Jesus _____

_____

_____

_____

135

For Further Study:
See Psalm 23:1;
Isaiah 25:6-9; Ezekiel
34:11-16, 23-31 for
lessons we can learn
through the miracle of
the loaves and fishes.

the disciples _____

_____

_____

_____

_____

10. Put yourself in the place of the five thousand.
    What implications does this incident have for
    your life?

    _____

    _____

    _____

    _____

    _____

    _____

11. Now put yourself in the place of the disciples in
    9:1-17. How are the lessons they learned also
    lessons you could apply? Write down one way in
    which each of the following is significant for
    you:

    Jesus' attitudes _____

    _____

    _____

    _____

    _____

    Jesus' identity and power _____

    _____

    _____

    _____

    _____

the disciples own mission, and how they should
carry it out

_____

_____

_____

_____

_____

_____

12. Does any of this prompt you to respond in some
practical way? If so, describe what you plan to
do or pray persistently about.

_____

_____

_____

_____

_____

_____

13. Summarize what 9:1-17 has to do with the message of the Gospel.

_____

_____

_____

_____

_____

14. List any questions you have about 9:1-17.

_____

_____

_____

_____

For the group

Warm-up. Ask if anyone in the group has ever done evangelism with strangers. Let each person who has done this tell one thing he or she learned from the experience.

Read Aloud.

Summarize.

Questions. One task in studying 9:1-17 is to decide what aspects were relevant only to Jesus' original disciples, what aspects are relevant only to the disciples and some modern Christian workers, and what aspects are relevant to everyone who wants to work for God's Kingdom. For instance, is 9:1-2 a universal mission? Is 9:3 a universal approach to mass evangelism? Two safeguards you can use for sound application are:

1. Observe and interpret the passage carefully before you venture into application. What was Jesus trying to teach *the original disciples* with each command and experience?
2. State explicitly how your situation is comparable to the disciples' and how it is different. A command or principle in Scripture is applicable to you to the extent that your situation is comparable to the original one.

With these guidelines in mind, you should be able to glean lessons for your own discipleship.

Summarize.

Evaluation. If you have extra discussion time, you can always use it to share results of your efforts to apply Luke's Gospel. "Results" does not mean that you should be able to prove how you have changed dramatically in just a few weeks. Rather, it means that you should be able to describe new insights you have had, changes in your attitudes or prayer lives, or even results of trying to turn the other cheek or give sacrificially.

Some group members may feel unable to apply 9:1-17 or other passages on their own. But notice that Jesus considered a small group of disciples to be the first place to begin applying His teaching. How could you practice actively loving each other

138

or spreading the good news together? Plan at least one group application, to see if you find it helpful.

Wrap-up. If you are planning to go straight from lesson twelve to lesson thirteen, be sure you have enough copies of Volume Two of this study guide.

Worship. Thank God for inviting you to share in Jesus' mission to feed, heal, and proclaim the Kingdom. Ask Him to increase your willingness to be empowered, trained, and sent on this mission. Thank Him for being a God who provides abundantly for your every need.

1. Morris, page 164.
2. *The NIV Study Bible*, page 1506.
3. Wilcock, page 108.

LUKE 9:18-50

Christhood Clarified

Jesus' disciples have heard and learned His message of the Kingdom, and they have seen Him perform the signs of the Kingdom. The Twelve have even preached the message and performed the signs themselves. More than anyone else, these people have witnessed Jesus' character, ministry, and message. Now Jesus confronts them with the question that everyone is asking, from the crowds to Herod (9:7-9): Who is Jesus?

By now the disciples should really understand Jesus' mission and their own. But do they? Read 9:18-50 again, prayerfully.

Who is Jesus? (9:18-27)

1. How does the disciples' understanding of Jesus exceed that of the crowds?

what the crowds think (9:18-19) _____

_____

_____

_____

what the disciples think (9:20) _____

_____

_____

Warned them not to tell (9:21). "The people had
false notions about the Messiah and needed to
be taught further before Jesus identified himself
explicitly to the public. He had a crucial schedule to keep and could not be interrupted by
premature reactions."[1]

Son of Man (9:22). "Jesus' most common title for
himself. . . . In Daniel 7:13-14 the Son of Man
is pictured as a heavenly figure who in the end
times is entrusted by God with authority, glory
and sovereign power."[2] God calls Ezekiel "son of
man" (Ezekiel 33:2), so the title also suggests
that Jesus is a prophet, fully human, and a
representative of humanity before God.

2. What impression has Jesus given so far about
what it means to be the Christ? (Consider a few
of these verses: 5:20,24,32; 6:5,20-22,46;
7:14,22,48; 8:24,28-32,44,53-56; 9:16-17.)

_____

_____

_____

_____

_____

_____

3. What new aspect of Christhood does Jesus want
the disciples to understand (9:22)?

_____

_____

_____

_____

_____

4. Recall 6:40. What does Jesus' mission (9:22)
imply for His disciples (9:23-24)?

142

_____

_____

_____

_____

_____

Take up his cross (9:23). Crucifixion was a common way in which the Romans executed slaves and lower class people. In the cities of Palestine, condemned men were frequently seen carrying heavy wooden crossbeams to the place of execution. Thus, the disciples knew that a man carrying a crossbeam was going to suffer and die.

5. Name one way in which a modern Christian may be tempted to "save his life" (9:24).

_____

_____

_____

_____

_____

_____

6. Why must a disciple take care to deny himself and lose his life (9:24-26)?

_____

_____

_____

_____

_____

143

7. This week, how could you deny yourself and take up your cross daily? Think of one or two specific ways, and pray about them.

_____

_____

_____

_____

_____

Some (9:27). Probably the disciples, who had responded to Jesus by denying their personal desires and following Jesus. The evidence they were going to see would begin at the Transfiguration and continue through Jesus' resurrection, Pentecost, and the beginning of the Church.[3]

The Transfiguration (9:28-36)

Pray (9:28). Jesus prayed after ministering (4:42), before choosing His disciples (6:12), before asking them who He was (9:18), and now before His Transfiguration.

Moses and Elijah (9:30). Both men had left the world in unusual ways, and both "were regarded as types of figures to appear at the end of the age."[4] The Law required two witnesses to certify the truth of anything (Deuteronomy 19:15, Matthew 18:16); Moses the lawgiver represented the witness of the Law to Jesus, and Elijah represented the witness of the Prophets. Also, their presence proved that Jesus was neither Moses nor Elijah reborn, but greater than both, for He was going to fulfill both their ministries.

Glory (9:31-32). The splendor of God's presence (Exodus 33:18-23; 34:1-7,29-35; 40:34-38).

144

Shelters (9:33). Temporary structures, something between a tent and a hut. Perhaps Peter thought the three men were going to stay for some time on the mountain.

Cloud (9:34). The glory of the Lord appearing in the same form as when it descended on Mt. Sinai, when Moses entered it to receive the Law of God (Exodus 24:15-18).

For Thought and Discussion: a. What "departure" (Greek: *exodos*) was Jesus going to fulfill at Jerusalem (9:31)?

b. How did Peter's offer to build shelters reflect a misunderstanding of that "departure"?

For Thought and Discussion: Why is it important for us to know about the Transfiguration? Does it have significance for us today?

8. Explain the meaning of the Father's witness to Jesus (9:35). What was the Father trying to tell the disciples? (Consider what Jesus was "chosen" to be.)

_____

_____

_____

_____

_____

9. A week earlier, Peter had identified Jesus as the Messiah. Jesus had tried to clarify what fulfilling that role would mean and what loyalty to such a Messiah would require. What did the disciples learn about the Messiah from this mountaintop experience?

_____

_____

_____

_____

_____

A deliverance and a perplexing promise (9:37-45)

10. Why were Jesus' disciples unable to cast out the evil spirit (Luke 9:41, Mark 9:28-29)?

_____

For Further Study:
Compare Luke
9:37-45 to Mark
9:14-32.

**For Thought and
Discussion:** a. In
light of what the dis-
ciples had seen
(9:28-36), why did
they fail to under-
stand Jesus' predic-
tion (9:44-45)?

b. Why do you
suppose they were
afraid to ask for more
explanation (9:45)?

11. Jesus first predicted His rejection, execution,
and resurrection after Peter acclaimed Him
Christ (9:22). Then, a week later He predicted
His betrayal even while the people were marvel-
ing at His power over demons (9:43-44). What
might Jesus have been trying to teach the disciples by timing His predictions alongside those
events?

_____

_____

_____

_____

An argument (9:46-50)

Having failed to understand Jesus' prediction of suffering and betrayal, and having been afraid to admit
their obtuseness, the disciples begin to argue.

12. What were they arguing about (9:46)?

_____

_____

_____

13. In your own words, explain Jesus' response
(9:47-48).

_____

_____

_____

_____

_____

14. How does the disciples' argument show yet again their misconceptions of Christhood and discipleship (9:20-26,44-45,48)?

_____

_____

_____

_____

_____

15. It is ironic that 9:49 follows a correction of the disciples' competitive spirit. What attitude toward outsiders does Jesus teach in 9:50?

_____

_____

_____

_____

Your response

16. Summarize what 9:1-50 says about the mission and identity of . . .

the Christ (9:16,22,29-32,35,42,44)

_____

_____

_____

_____

_____

Optional Application: Meditate on one of Jesus' responses to the disciples' misunderstandings. Write down ways it applies to you.

For Thought and Discussion: a. What might it mean to "welcome" (NASB: "receive") a child in Jesus' name (9:48)?
   b. Why would welcoming a child in Jesus' name be equivalent to welcoming Jesus?

For Thought and Discussion: Review the disciples' failures in 9:18-50. Why were these men in need of more training?

For Further Study: In your outline, write how 9:1-50 culminates the first part of Luke's Gospel and shows why more training of the disciples (9:51-19:44) and the Crucifixion (19:45-24:53) will be necessary.

His disciples (9:1-6,13-17,23-26,48,50)

_____

_____

_____

_____

_____

17. a. Consider the disciples' failures in 9:33, 40-41,44-45,49-50. Do these or any other insights from 9:18-50 suggest an aspect of discipleship in which you would like to grow? If so, what is that aspect?

_____

_____

_____

_____

_____

b. Plan to memorize and meditate on any relevant verses. How else could you pursue growth or take action in this area?

_____

_____

_____

_____

_____

_____

18. List any questions you have about 9:18-50.

_____

_____

_____

_____

For the group

Warm-up. Ask, "What has been the toughest part of being a Christian for you this past week?"

Questions. In lessons two through eleven we looked at the content of the gospel (who Jesus is and what His message is) and the response He desires (what it means to be a disciple). This lesson culminates both of these themes, so keep both in mind as you study the details of the scenes.

If you have been unable to fully absorb and apply what Jesus has said about Himself and our response, you may be encouraged to observe in 9:18-50 that His disciples, who had been with Him personally for a year or more, also had a weak grasp of these things. They understood about Jesus' power, but not about the Cross. How are we like them? What advantages and resources do we have that they lacked? How can we learn from their mistakes? Since the disciples were a small group like you, how can you apply 9:46-50 within or outside your group?

Wrap-up. If your group is feeling the need for a temporary change of pace, this is a natural point at which to take a break from Luke for a week or two. You can devote a meeting to praying and sharing, have dinner together, plan a group application of something you've learned, or study something totally different such as some psalms. If you pause for more than two weeks, urge the group to reread 1:1-9:50 before beginning lesson thirteen. Much of Parts Two and Three (9:51-24:53) presuppose the context of what has gone before.

Worship. Praise Jesus for what 9:18-50 reveals about Him, about what it means to be the Christ. Praise Him for His power, His glory, and His suffering. Thank Him for inviting you to share in all of this.

1. *The NIV Study Bible*, page 1557.
2. *The NIV Study Bible*, page 1510.
3. Marshall, pages 377-379.
4. Marshall, page 380

STUDY AIDS

For further information on the material covered in this study, consider the following sources. If your local bookstore does not have them, you can ask the bookstore to order them from the publishers, or find them in a public, university, or seminary library.

Commentaries on Luke

Geldenhuys, Norval. *The Gospel of Luke* (New International Commentary on the New Testament, Eerdmans, 1951).
    Scholarly; readable for laymen; less thorough than Marshall, but also less expensive and lengthy. Offers the insight of Dutch scholars not often noted by English writers.

Hendriksen, William. *Luke* (New Testament Commentary, Baker, 1978).
    An expository, or sermon-like, approach to verse-by-verse commentary. Very readable and inspiring. Separates analysis of the Greek from the main exposition to avoid troubling the layman. Each section includes "Practical Lessons"—suggestions of how the passage applies today.

Marshall, I. Howard. *The Gospel of Luke* (New International Greek Testament Commentary, Eerdmans, 1978).
    The most thorough and up-to-date commentary on Luke's Gospel now available. Exceptionally readable, despite its length and the number of references. Ignorance of Greek should not hinder anyone willing to tackle a long book, but this book is especially useful if you are just researching a particular passage.

Morris, Leon. *The Gospel According to Saint Luke* (Tyndale New Testamant Commentary, Eerdmans, 1974).

Concise and well-researched, and available in an inexpensive paperback edition. An ordinary person can read straight through this one for good background, cross-references, and comments. Morris omits most of the critical discussions of sources, parallels in the other Gospels, etc. that Marshall and Geldenhuys address.

Wilcock, Michael. *Savior of the World* (The Bible Speaks Today Series, Inter-Varsity, 1979.)
Not a verse-by-verse analysis like the above, but instead exposition of each passage with excellent application to the present day. Wilcock is especially good at fitting a particular passage into the train of thought of the chapter and the themes of the whole book. The scholarship is kept in the background. This is an inexpensive paperback.

Historical Sources

Bruce, F. F. *New Testament History* (Doubleday, 1971).
A readable history of Herodian kings, Roman governors, philosophical schools, Jewish sects, Jesus, the early Jerusalem church, Paul, and early gentile Christianity. Well-documented with footnotes for the serious student, but the notes do not intrude.

Edersheim, Alfred. *The Life and Times of Jesus the Messiah* (Eerdmans, 1971).
Reprint of the classic two-volume original (second edition) of 1886. Some of the material is out of date, but most is still sound. The prose of this life of Jesus is of timeless value. Edersheim was a converted Jew, and his knowledge of the Jewish law makes this book outstanding.

Harrison, E. F. *Introduction to the New Testament* (Eerdmans, 1971).
History from Alexander the Great—who made Greek culture dominant in the biblical world—through philosophies, pagan and Jewish religion, Jesus' ministry and teaching, and the spread of Christianity. Very good maps and photographs of the land, art, and architecture of New Testament times.

Concordances, Dictionaries, and Handbooks

A *concordance* lists words of the Bible alphabetically along with each verse in which the word appears. It lets you do your own word studies. An *exhaustive* concordance lists every word used in a given translation, while an *abridged* or *complete* concordance omits either some words, some occurrences of the word, or both.
The two best exhaustive concordances are *Strong's Exhaustive Concordance* and *Young's Analytical Concordance to the Bible*. Both are available based on the King James Version of the Bible and the New American Stand-

ard Bible. *Strong's* has an index by which you can find out which Greek or Hebrew word is used in a given English verse. *Young's* breaks up each English word it translates. However, neither concordance requires knowledge of the original language.

Among other good, less expensive concordances, *Cruden's Complete Concordance* is keyed to the King James and Revised Versions, and *The NIV Complete Concordance* is keyed to the New International Version. These include all references to every word included, but they omit "minor" words. They also lack indexes to the original languages.

A **Bible dictionary** or **Bible encyclopedia** alphabetically lists articles about people, places, doctrines, important words, customs, and geography of the Bible.

The New Bible Dictionary, edited by J. D. Douglas, F. F. Bruce, J. I. Packer, N. Hillyer, D. Guthrie, A. R. Millard, and D. J. Wiseman (Tyndale, 1982) is more comprehensive than most dictionaries. Its 1300 pages include quantities of information along with excellent maps, charts, diagrams, and an index for cross-referencing.

Unger's Bible Dictionary by Merrill F. Unger (Moody, 1979) is equally good and is available in an inexpensive paperback edition.

The Zondervan Pictorial Encyclopedia edited by Merrill C. Tenney (Zondervan, 1975, 1976) is excellent and exhaustive, and is being revised and updated in the 1980's. However, its five 1000-page volumes are a financial investment, so all but very serious students may prefer to use it at a church, public, college, or seminary library.

Unlike a Bible dictionary in the above sense, *Vine's Expository Dictionary of New Testament Words* by W. E. Vine (various publishers) alphabetically lists major words used in the King James Version and defines each New Testament Greek word that KJV translates with that English word. *Vine's* lists verse references where that Greek word appears, so that you can do your own cross-references and word studies without knowing any Greek.

Vine's is a good basic book for beginners, but it is much less complete than other Greek helps for English speakers. More serious students might prefer *The New International Dictionary of New Testament Theology*, edited by Colin Brown (Zondervan) or *The Theological Dictionary of the New Testament* by Gerhard Kittel and Gerhard Friedrich, abridged in one volume by Geoffrey W. Bromiley (Eerdmans).

A **Bible atlas** can be a great aid to understanding what is going on in a book of the Bible and how geography affected events. Here are a few good choices:

The MacMillan Atlas by Yohanan Aharoni and Michael Avi-Yonah (MacMillan, 1968, 1977) contains 264 maps, 89 photos, and 12 graphics. The many maps of individual events portray battles, movements of people, and changes of boundaries in detail.

The New Bible Atlas by J. J. Bimson and J. P. Kane (Tyndale, 1985) has 73 maps, 34 photos, and 34 graphics. Its evangelical perspective, concise and helpful text, and excellent research make it a very good choice, but its greatest strength is its outstanding graphics, such as cross-sections of the Dead Sea.

The Bible Mapbook by Simon Jenkins (Lion, 1984) is much shorter and less expensive than most other atlases, so it offers a good first taste of the usefulness of maps. It contains 91 simple maps, very little text, and 20 graphics. Some of the graphics are computer-generated and intriguing.

The Moody Atlas of Bible Lands by Barry J. Beitzel (Moody, 1984) is scholarly, very evangelical, and full of theological text, indexes, and references. This admirable reference work will be too deep and costly for some, but Beitzel shows vividly how God prepared the land of Israel perfectly for the acts of salvation He was going to accomplish in it.

A **handbook** of biblical customs can also be useful. Some good ones are *Today's Handbook of Bible Times and Customs* by William L. Coleman (Bethany, 1984) and the less detailed *Daily Life in Bible Times* (Nelson, 1982).

For Small Group Leaders

How to Lead Small Group Bible Studies (NavPress, 1982).
> Just 71 pages. It hits the highlights of how to get members acquainted, ask questions, plan lessons, deal with interpersonal relations, and handle prayer.

The Small Group Leader's Handbook by Steve Barker et al. (InterVarsity, 1982).
> Written by an InterVarsity small group with college students primarily in mind. It includes more than the above book on small group dynamics and how to lead in light of them, and many ideas for worship, building community, and outreach. It has a good chapter on doing inductive Bible study.

Getting Together: A Guide for Good Groups by Em Griffin (InterVarsity, 1982).
> Applies to all kinds of groups, not just Bible studies. From his own experience, Griffin draws deep insights into why people join groups; how people relate to each other; and principles of leadership, decision-making, and discussions. It is fun to read, but its 229 pages will take more time than the above books.

You Can Start a Bible Study Group by Gladys Hunt (Harold Shaw, 1984).
> Builds on Hunt's thirty years of experience leading groups. This book is wonderfully focused on God's enabling. It is both clear and applicable for Bible study groups of all kinds.

The Small Group Letter (NavPress).
> Unique. Its six pages per issue, ten issues per year are packed with

practical ideas for asking questions, planning Bible studies, leading discussions, dealing with group dynamics, encouraging spiritual growth, doing outreach, and so on. It stays up to date because writers always discuss what they are currently doing as small group members and leaders. To subscribe, write to *The Small Group Letter*, Subscription Services, Post Office Box 1164, Dover, New Jersey 07801.

Bible Study Methods

Braga, James. *How to Study the Bible* (Multnomah, 1982).
    Clear chapters on a variety of approaches to Bible study: synthetic, geographical, cultural, historical, doctrinal, practical, and so on. Designed to help the ordinary person without seminary training to use these approaches.

Fee, Gordon, and Douglas Stuart. *How to Read the Bible For All Its Worth* (Zondervan, 1982).
    After explaining in general what interpretation (exegesis) and application (hermeneutics) are, Fee and Stuart offer chapters on interpreting and applying the different kinds of writing in the Bible: Epistles, Gospels, Old Testament Law, Old Testament narrative, the Prophets, Psalms, Wisdom, and Revelation. Fee and Stuart also suggest good commentaries on each biblical book. They write as evangelical scholars who personally recognize Scripture as God's Word for their daily lives.

Jensen, Irving L. *Independent Bible Study* (Moody, 1963), and *Enjoy Your Bible* (Moody, 1962).
    The former is a comprehensive introduction to the inductive Bible study method, expecially the use of synthetic charts. The latter is a simpler introduction to the subject.

Wald, Oletta. *The Joy of Discovery in Bible Study* (Augsburg, 1975).
    Wald focuses on issues such as how to observe all that is in a text, how to ask questions of a text, how to use grammar and passage structure to see the writer's point, and so on. Very helpful on these subjects.